PRAISE FOR ANGIE WYNNE
and BabyCheapskate.com

"Angie Wynne, of Atlanta, is a mom with a purpose: She single-mindedly tracks all the latest deals on diapers, formula, and other baby necessities and posts the finds on her Web site, BabyCheapskate.com. One minute on her site can save you hours of shopping around—and lots of cash!"

—*Parents* Magazine

"Find discounts on all your parenting needs at BabyCheap skate.com, which scours the Web for the best deals every week." —*All You*

"Why you'll 'like' it: Another money-saving page, with baby bargains, product reviews, and links to great deals. The page also features top diaper and formula deals of the week. What parents talk about: Gift ideas, which products are best for traveling (Pack 'n Plays and Britax car seats, in their opinion), and input on other sites to find baby items on sale."

—Babble, which included Baby Cheapskate in its
Top 50 Facebook Fan Pages for Parents

"If you have a baby, or are shopping for a baby, or even know a baby, you need to know Baby Cheapskate. I head here every week to find out where to get the best deals on diapers."

—Mom Central

D1303271

THE BABY CHEAPSKATE
Guide to Bargains

• • •

How to Save on Blankets, Bottles,
and Everything Baby

ANGELA WYNNE

NEW AMERICAN LIBRARY

NEW AMERICAN LIBRARY
Published by New American Library, a division of
Penguin Group (USA) Inc., 375 Hudson Street,
New York, New York 10014, USA
Penguin Group (Canada), 90 Eglinton Avenue East, Suite 700, Toronto,
Ontario M4P 2Y3, Canada (a division of Pearson Penguin Canada Inc.)
Penguin Books Ltd., 80 Strand, London WC2R 0RL, England
Penguin Ireland, 25 St. Stephen's Green, Dublin 2,
Ireland (a division of Penguin Books Ltd.)
Penguin Group (Australia), 250 Camberwell Road, Camberwell, Victoria 3124,
Australia (a division of Pearson Australia Group Pty. Ltd.)
Penguin Books India Pvt. Ltd., 11 Community Centre, Panchsheel Park,
New Delhi - 110 017, India
Penguin Group (NZ), 67 Apollo Drive, Rosedale, Auckland 0632,
New Zealand (a division of Pearson New Zealand Ltd.)
Penguin Books (South Africa) (Pty.) Ltd., 24 Sturdee Avenue,
Rosebank, Johannesburg 2196, South Africa

Penguin Books Ltd., Registered Offices:
80 Strand, London WC2R 0RL, England

First published by New American Library,
a division of Penguin Group (USA) Inc.

First Printing, May 2012
10 9 8 7 6 5 4 3 2 1

 REGISTERED TRADEMARK—MARCA REGISTRADA

LIBRARY OF CONGRESS CATALOGING-IN-PUBLICATION DATA:
Wynne, Angela.
The baby cheapskate guide to bargains: how to save on blankets, bottles, and everything baby/Angela Wynne.
p.   cm.
ISBN 978-0-451-23669-2 (pbk.)
1. Infants' supplies—Purchasing.   2. Consumer education.   I. Title.
RJ61.W96   2012
649'.122068—dc23   2011047207

Set in Granjon
Designed by Patrice Sheridan

Printed in the United States of America

PUBLISHER'S NOTE
Publisher and Author have exercised reasonable care to ensure that the information contained in the Work is complete and accurate. However, neither Publisher nor Author is engaged in rendering professional advice or services and accordingly both expressly disclaim all representations and warranties with respect to the completeness, accuracy and/or suitability of any information, ideas, opinions, procedures, and suggestions contained in the Work. Notwithstanding anything to the contrary elsewhere in this Agreement, neither Publisher nor Author shall be liable or responsible for any liability, loss, injury or damage allegedly arising from any information, ideas, opinions, procedures, and suggestions contained in the Work.

While the author has made every effort to provide accurate telephone numbers, Internet addresses and other contact information at the time of publication, neither the publisher nor the author assumes any responsibility for errors, or for changes that occur after publication. Further, publisher does not have any control over and does not assume any responsibility for author or third-party web sites or their content.

Contents

• • •

Acknowledgments   *xi*

Introduction   *xiii*

Part 1: Baby Savings 101   1

Chapter 1

Saving Big: The Basics   **3**

Why Do We Buy?   4

What Kind of Saver Are You?   9

5 Principles of Saving Big   10

Chapter 2

**Building Your Shopping List and
Finding Big Discounts**   **25**

Do Your Research Before You Shop   26

How Low Will It Go: Tracking Prices   30

Get the Scoop on Sales, Clearance, and Closeouts   35

Contents

What About Warehouse Clubs:
Are They Worth It?   38

Saving with Social Media   40

Chapter 3

Creating the Registry: From Woombies to Onesies   45

Where Will You Register?   46

Be Smart: Register for the Essentials   49

It's Raining Freebies: Baby Showers   56

Chapter 4

Saving Big with Coupons   61

Couponing Basics for the Absolute Beginner   62

On the Hunt: The Best Coupon Sources   65

Loyalty Cards, Rebates, and Vouchers:
Three More Cost Cutters   72

3 Ways to Take Couponing Even Further   76

Part 2: Life's Little Necessities   79

Chapter 5

Setting Up the Nursery: Cool Cribs and More   81

5 Basic Ideas for Nursery Planning   82

7 Space-maximizing Tips for a Mini Nursery   83

Designing the Nursery: Inspiration and Advice   85

Crib Notes: How to Buy a Great Crib for Less   89

Contents

Bedding: Bye-Bye Bumpers and Other Tips   95
Pretty It Up: Decor and Nursery Furniture   99
Planning a Nursery for Multiples   108

Chapter 6

Feeding Baby for Less: From Boobies to Bananas   113

Breastfeeding and Nursing Accessories   114
The Secret Formula for Saving on
   Baby Formula   125
Fill 'Er Up: The Best Baby Bottles   131
Baby Food: No Silver Spoon Required   134
High Chairs: Do You Really Need One?   138

Chapter 7

Diapering: The Bottom Line   145

Cloth Diapering 101   146
Disposable Diaper Basics   153
3 Rules That Can Save You Hundreds on
   Premium Diapers   158
What About the Wipes?   164

Chapter 8

Changing Time: Bags, Pails, and Other Diapering Doodads   169

Mama Needs a Brand-new Bag (or Does She?):
   Diaper Bags   170

Contents

Diaper Pails: The Straight Poop 177

Dealing with Diaper Rash 181

Chapter 9

Coming Clean:
Baby and the Bathwater **185**

Rub-a-Dub-Dub: How to Save on a Tub 186

Soaps and Shampoos: Tear-free Shopping 191

Towels That Won't Leave Your Wallet High
and Dry 193

Make a Splash: Bath Toys 194

Chapter 10
Sizing Up Your Baby Clothing Needs **197**

Hooray for Free Baby Clothes! 199

What Does a Newborn Need, Anyway? 199

Layette for Less 200

Sizing It Up and Stocking Up 210

This Little Piggy: Baby's First Shoes 213

Resell and Recoup the Cost 216

Part 3: Gear and Other Goodies **219**

Chapter 11
Cruising: Car Seats 101 **221**

Car Seats: A Crash Course 223

Choosing and Saving on Infant Car Seats   227
Convertible Car Seats: Safety and Savings   231

Chapter 12

Hoofing It: Strollers and Baby Carriers   235

Strollers   236
Baby Carriers   247

Chapter 13

Gearing Up:
Bouncers, Bassinets, and More   257

A Play Yard Playbook   258
Will Your Baby Be a Swinger or a Bouncer?   263
Rock On, Baby: Rockers   268
Bassinets, Cradles, and Moses Baskets   269
Bumbo and BébéPOD: A Different Kind
of Babysitter   270

Chapter 14

Choosing Drool-worthy First Toys   273

Tummy-time Fun: Activity Mats and
Baby Gyms   276
Classic First Toys Your Baby Will
Go Gaga For   276
Stationary Activity Centers:
Plastic Mega Hunks of Fun   284
Bouncing Baby Boys and Girls: Jumpers   287

Contents

Books, Music, and Other Media for Your
    Little Mogul   289
Out and About with Bambino   292

Appendix A:
100+ Helpful Web Sites for Smart Shoppers   *295*
Appendix B:
Smart Products to Put on Your Baby Registry   *301*
Index   *303*

Acknowledgments

• • •

I'd like to offer my heartfelt thanks to some wonderful people, without whom this book would not have been possible: To my agent, Chris Park, who with her question about whether I had ever thought about writing a book got the whole ball rolling. And to my editor, Mark Chait at NAL, for his belief in the idea of the book and for his expert guidance. To my mom, Sharon Atcheson, the original cheapskate and master shopper who, much to my consternation as a teen, schooled in me the basics of frugality that form the foundation of my blog and this book. To my husband, Peter, and my son, Nate, without whom there would be no blog and no book at all. To the countless readers who have taught me so much about parenting and community. And to the chorus of moms who contributed their suggestions, stories, thoughts, and wisdom to this book.

Introduction

• • •

If you're like me, the first thing you did when you found out you were pregnant was grab some baby magazines. Well, the first thing I did was turn really pale and sit down on the toilet. The second thing I did was tell the baby's daddy. And then there was the obligatory OB appointment. But grabbing as many baby magazines as I could get my hands on (and smuggle out of the OB's waiting room) was right up there on the list.

These magazines were filled with advertisements for the latest, greatest, "must-have" baby products, all carefully worded to convince you that no mother in her right mind would attempt parenthood without them. If a weighted, hand-shaped pillow was going to help my newborn sleep through the night (hah!), then by golly it was for me. Only later, after the euphoria of my pregnancy had faded a little, did the sticker shock set in.

Babies. Are. Expensive. Period. A 2009 U.S. Department of Agriculture study sets the price tag of a baby born into a middle-income family in the United States at more than $23,000 for the first two years. That's nearly $1,000 a month spent on housing, food, transportation, clothing, health care, child care, and other expenses (get your own estimate at www.cnpp.usda.gov/calculatorintro.htm). What's more, many families' budgets take a double hit as they shift from a two-income household to a one-income household should one parent choose to stay at home to care for the child(ren).

The good news? That figure is much, much higher than it needs to be. Why? Because rookie parents too often lack the benefit of experienced parents' cost-cutting wisdom. They buy things they don't need and pay too much for things they do need. They are forced to learn the secrets of saving on baby through trial and error.

That was the case for my husband and me. The initial feeling of joy at our impending parenthood quickly gave way to the shock of discovering that diapers and formula (should we use it) would cost more per month than our car payment. Since we were self-employed and bringing in rather modest paychecks, a baby had the potential to be a serious budget buster for us.

Luckily, I grew up shopping with a mother for whom finding a great deal is a sport, and that thrill of scoring a hot bargain rubbed off on me (thanks, Mom!). Buying quality baby stuff at big discounts quickly became a personal challenge.

After our son was born, I'd sit my harried, unshowered, sleep-deprived self on the couch each week with the Sunday paper ad circulars, a pair of scissors, and a calculator, clipping coupons and scoping out the best sales on diapers and formula. If only, I thought, there was a way to access all of this information quickly. It was 2005, and to my knowledge, there wasn't. Since I was doing all the groundwork already, I figured the least I could do would be to post my frugal finds online to help other cash-strapped new parents save some dough and oh-so-valuable time.

This desire to pass on my own hard-won baby savings know-how gave birth to my blog, BabyCheapskate.com. Through my years spent researching sales, products, and brands for Baby Cheapskate, I've learned that it's possible to cut costs without cutting corners. Armed with a little shopping savvy, you can indeed give your baby the best, and you can do it for less.

The name of the blog, Baby Cheapskate, thumbs its nose at the notion that you need to spend a fortune during your baby's first year. In truth, I'm not a cheapskate. To folks who like to spend more money than they have to, I may seem like one. In truth, I'm simply a smart shopper. I want you to be a smart shopper, too.

Baby Cheapskate struck a chord with parents early on, and its popularity only grew as the United States entered the "Great Recession." Today, it's the most popular baby-bargain blog of its kind, receiving more than three quarters of a million hits per month. The site's Facebook fan page has nearly fifty thousand fans at the time of this writing.

But I can't take all the credit. Part of the value of Baby Cheapskate, to me, is that it's a group effort. Since 2005, I've posted deals and parents have responded in kind, sharing with me—and each other—ideas about what you need for a baby and what you can skip. They've imparted their wisdom about when you should scrimp and when you should splurge, about not spending more than you have to on all that's destined to be peed on, pooped in, and worn twice before it's outgrown, and so very much more. I'll be sharing some of these parents' advice and stories with you in this book. After all, learning from the successes and challenges of other families is a heck of a lot easier than going it alone.

In an ideal world, all your baby's material needs would be met through generous gifts at lovely pastel-ballooned baby showers. Nothing's better than free, right? But in most cases it doesn't work out that way, and you end up picking up the tab largely on your own, especially for baby number two, number three, and so on, who may not get baby showers. That's why I've created this little guide to saving big bucks on baby stuff.

The book is divided into three parts. In the first part, Baby Savings 101, I'll teach you the basics of saving—couponing, shopping the sales, and more. That way you'll have a good foundation for the savings ideas we'll be discussing later in the book.

In the second part of the book, Life's Little Necessities, we'll focus on items you'll use from day to day as you meet your baby's basic needs. You'll learn about all the baby stuff you may want for baby care at home—including diapering, feeding, buying baby clothes, and setting up the nursery.

The third part of the book, Gear and Other Goodies, steps beyond meeting these basic needs. It discusses gear you'll use outside the home, like car seats, strollers, and carriers. You'll get the scoop on baby gear like swings and bouncers, too. In the final chapter I'll share what I know about choosing fun stuff like toys and entertainment.

Within each chapter, you'll hear from fifty-plus real parents who contributed stories and tips to this book. You'll also find creative ideas for taking your savings even further, along with "Quick and Easy" savings ideas for when you want to cut costs without spending much effort or time. The payoff? If you follow the advice laid out in this book, you can expect to shave 30 percent and more off the cost of preparing for baby.

Congratulations on your new family. You have a wonderful journey ahead of you. Now let's save some money.

PART ONE

· ·

Baby Savings 101

Saving Big:
The Basics

The 2010 documentary *Babies* follows four adorable babies from around the world through roughly the first year of their lives. One of the babies, Ponijao from Namibia, lives in conditions that most Westerners would consider primitive. He crawls around in the dirt, and most of the time he's naked or wearing a loincloth. The family doesn't own a single "baby item"—no diapers, crib, or stroller to be found. I was struck by how little Ponijao needed to thrive—and thrive he did—in the company of his loving family.

Of course, Ponijao's world is pretty foreign to most of us. I'm guessing you're not reading this book in a hut in Namibia but rather in a place where creature comforts are a lot more commonplace. If I'm right, the chances that you'll raise your baby without buying a single baby item are pretty slim indeed.

The journey to saving begins with the recognition that you don't need to spend nearly as much as you think you do. Of course, anyone who's ever tried to cut out junk food has found that it's easy to say you'll just have a *tiny* bite of that delicious chocolate cake on the counter, but much harder to actually resist grabbing a plate and a fork and digging in.

Walking into a baby department store is a lot like walking into a bakery at lunchtime. The aisles are packed with thousands of tantalizing gadgets and doodads that promise to add pleasure and comfort to your life. And there are even a few free samples to make sure you consume.

Why Do We Buy?

So why do we buy? Babies don't care how many cute outfits they have, what brand of stroller their mom pushes them in, or how trendy their nursery is. It's parents who do, and the multibillion-dollar baby product industry wants to make sure they spend as much as possible, despite their best budget intentions.

Quite simply, new and expectant parents are a marketer's gold mine that dozens (if not hundreds) of baby industry retailers, manufacturers, and service providers can't wait to dig into. Marketers study parents' social media interactions on Twitter and other sites, their buying behavior, their survey responses, their birth announcements, and other data to pinpoint precisely which marketing materials to push to them and when.

The result? Soon-to-be parents, particularly mothers, are hit full force with a barrage of advertising from a dozen different directions from the first time they open a parenting magazine to their baby's first visit to the pediatrician and beyond. Often the advertising arrives in the guise of "helpful information" for new parents—e-mail newsletters, blog reviews, and so on. Info-thirsty expectant parents who lack more experienced moms and dads to turn to for advice are particularly vulnerable to these advertorials.

Reader Tips

The baby magazines always have lists of "must-haves" coupled with special features explaining the need for all of these items. I didn't have many "Mom" friends and it's scary having a baby, what else did I have to rely on for advice?

—Michelle

Another popular way that baby product manufacturers get the word out about their products is through gift bags and welcome kits full of coupons, freebies, samples, and ads. Gift bag advertising is, in the words of the advertisers themselves, "ideal for encouraging trial and stimulating loyalty at a key product purchasing stage" (www

.meredith.com/mediakit/ab/print/abmk_fyolSam.html). And literature aimed at convincing brands to participate in gift bag programs says that the soon-to-be mom is "a woman at the most responsive lifestage" (http://bit.ly/gift bagprogram). The key to bringing in the bucks is to hook the soon-to-be mom on a brand or product "*before* she completes her baby registry" (http://bit.ly/giftbagprogram). Like when you buy your first pair of maternity jeans.

The maternity clothing store Motherhood Maternity gives shoppers (over 2 million of them, according to company advertising) a gift bag with the first in-store purchase of each pregnancy. In it you'll find coupons, samples, and a whole lot of advertising.

The "gift bags" and "welcome kits" don't stop there. Think your ob-gyn and pediatricians' offices are ad-free zones? Think again. The Parents Healthy Kids Sampler goes out to 1.6 million parents from eight thousand pediatricians' offices. And don't be surprised if you get another "goodie" bag when you leave the hospital with your new baby.

Two Types of Needs

There are a few reasons we're at our "most receptive life-stage" for advertising when a baby is about to come into our lives. Finding out that your family is growing is exciting, and we shop in anticipation. It goes deeper than that, though. To get back to my chocolate cake analogy, overspending, like overeating, is usually an attempt to meet a psychological or social need:

- **Psychological.** From the "what will it be like" stage before the baby is born to those crazy new-baby days, parenthood comes with a lot of uncertainty. "Retail therapy" comforts us and helps us feel in control. If we can just buy the right product our baby will sleep through the night/be fully potty trained by a year old/become a national chess champion at the age of three. . . . If only it worked that way.

- **Social.** As a culture, Americans are rarely content with what we have. We value consumption and competition. Some of us feel like if we're not giving our kids the latest model of the hottest baby items out there, we're somehow shortchanging them (or ourselves).

How to Avoid Impulse Spending

Avoiding impulsive and emotional spending is a lot like avoiding impulsive and emotional eating. In fact, the tips found in books and articles about eating less inspire the temptation-avoidance techniques below.

Evaluate the purpose of any baby product information you see. Recognize advertisements, free samples, and coupons for what they are—tools to encourage you to buy.

Keep a spending diary, and write down what you spend every time you buy something, no matter how small it is. This forces you to become conscious of what's actually happening. Write down *all* your purchases for a week. At the end of the week, go through each item on your list and think about how you feel about the purchase now. Do you regret it? Did it make you happy? If it was an impulsive purchase, think about what may have triggered it. Then try to avoid those triggers.

Realize that you don't need to be prepared for everything. It's great to have some extra diapers and wipes on hand so you don't run out, but don't go crazy stockpiling and buying ahead. Let an actual need arise . . . and then deal with it.

Baby Cheapskate reader Carrie puts it this way: "I wanted everything to be *just* right. No running out to the store or stressing out for any reason. It's just not reasonable or needed. So what if hubby comes home one night and has to go through the horrible process of running out for diapers! (Oh, the horrors!) I had to learn to go easier on myself. I run out of things for me, so why not give myself the same amount of slack as a first-time mom?"

Refuse to buy anything without a self-imposed "cooling off" period. When shopping online, try putting the item in your cart and then doing nothing. Wait a few hours (or days) before you buy. This gives you time to think about *why* you want to buy the item.

Set reasonable savings goals and spending limits and

post them near your computer or in your wallet so that you'll see them before you pull the trigger on a purchase. For example, "Crib: spend $250 or less" or "Don't buy unless it's 25 percent off or more." Make another list of temptation-busting questions like "Do I really need it?" and "What will happen if I don't buy it?" and keep it in your wallet, too. These reminders will help you keep your budgetary goals from flying out the window and will help you rein in the urge to buy on impulse.

So far I've told you how *not* to spend. But that's not really why you're reading this book. You've got babies on the mind (and perhaps one in the oven) and you've got some preparing to do.

So how do you get what you need and want without spending a thousand dollars a month on your baby? By arming yourself with the wisdom and tools you'll need to spend much, much less. Couponing gets all the press, but there are a number of tools that will benefit your budget. We'll talk about them later, but first, think about your savings priorities. How much work are you willing to put into saving money?

What Kind of Saver Are You?

I *know* you want to save money on baby items. Otherwise, you wouldn't be reading this, right? But where exactly do you fall on the saver's continuum? In truth, there's not one kind of bargain hunter. We all have different attitudes toward saving and spending, dictated by our upbringings, values, lifestyles, and income levels.

Some of us are minimalists and want to buy as little as possible, period. Others of us want our babies to have all the best stuff, but we want to pay as little as possible for it. Some of us are passionate bargain hunters who adore shopping and couponing. Some of us are creative DIY-ers and master "repurposers," and some of us simply want to find great deals without spending all day hunting for them.

Many of the savings tools we'll discuss here will jibe with your family's lifestyle and interests, and some may not. Whether you consider yourself an "extreme couponer" à la the TLC television show, or you simply want to pick up a few helpful tips, you're reading the right book. Each chapter will present options for making do with less, for quick and easy savings, and for going all out in your savings quest. Feel free to pick and choose. Do what works for your family.

5 Principles of Saving Big

Before we get into specifics about what baby gear to buy and when, let's go over the five basic principles of saving major bucks on baby stuff.

Principle 1: Needs and Wants Are Two Different Things

What do you really *need* for your baby? Did you know that the Babies"R"Us Registry "must-haves" list is over three hundred items long? Crazy, right? Do yourself a favor now. Throw out all the mental images and shopping lists you've no doubt started accumulating and repeat after me: "I need to meet my baby's basic needs."

If you want to spend the absolute minimum on baby stuff, only buy what you and your baby will need, and I do mean *need* on the most basic level. What are your baby's basic physiological needs (remember learning about those in high school?)? Sleep, health and well-being, food, safety and security, and clothing and shelter. You need to buy very few baby products to help meet those needs. Take a look at this breakdown:

- **Sleep.** Assuming you don't go the family bed route, you'll need a safe place for your baby to sleep—a crib, bassinet, cosleeper, and so on—and bedding to go with it.
- **Health and well-being.** You'll need diapers. Whether they're cloth or disposable is up to you. You'll also need something to clean your baby's bottom—cloth or disposable wipes—and somewhere sanitary to put dirty diapers.
- **Food.** If you breastfeed you'll benefit from having a

breast pump, especially if you'll be returning to work (you can express breast milk by hand, but it's not very efficient). You may also need bottles and nipples for expressed milk or formula.

- **Safety and security.** You'll need an infant or convertible car seat if you plan on driving with your baby.
- **Clothing and shelter.** You'll need blankets to swaddle and clothing to keep your baby warm. The specific items of clothing you need depend on the climate and temperature when your baby arrives.

It's pretty hard to imagine raising a baby in Western culture with only a place to sleep, diapers, wipes, and maybe a car seat and a breast pump, but this is really all you *need*.

Everything that isn't necessary in meeting your baby's basic physiological needs is a *want*. You don't *need* it. That includes many items that top retailers' "registry musthaves" lists: strollers, bouncers, swings, play yards, and all that cute nursery decor. In later chapters, I'll tell you which items are really, really nice to have, and which top parents' lists of "most useless baby product."

Principle 2: Get What You Can Without Spending a Dime

When it comes to saving money on baby items, you can't beat *free*. There are more reliable sources of free baby items than you may think, and we're not talking Dumpster diving, either.

Chances are, within five minutes of announcing to the world that you're expecting a baby, you'll be offered someone's gently used baby clothing, gear, or nursery items. Whether the gear is loaned or given, accept it (as long as it seems safe and in good condition, of course)! We were the lucky recipients of so many boxes of gently used baby clothing we didn't have to buy anything for over a year! We also received a bouncer, activity center, crib mirror, and mobile for free. Awesome!

Reader Heather got some good stuff, too. She writes, "I got quite a few secondhand things. I got a swing and a Bumbo seat from my brother-in-law's sister. I got an Ex-erSaucer and a jumper from my sister. All four items were in great condition and it was nice not to have to go out and buy all . . . these expensive items! My daughter loved the bouncer and being on the floor more than anything, so these items were only used a little bit, so I am glad we didn't buy them brand-new 'cause it would not have been worth it!"

Should those freebie offers be fewer or farther between than you'd like, there are a couple of online services you can turn to:

Check for Recalls on Secondhand Items

When considering used items, free or not, you'll want to make sure they haven't been recalled and that they meet current safety standards. Check for recalls at www.recalls.gov. It's a good idea to avoid used car seats, since you have no way of knowing whether they've been involved in a crash.

- **Freecycle.org** is probably the most well-known and widely available freebie source, with nearly five thousand local groups. Join your local group (search for one at www.freecycle.org) and you'll gain access to listings of free merchandise near you.

Sarah scored big on Freecycle. "I got a Little Tikes plastic slide for free through Freecycle. It has been used on nearly every sunny day since we got it five years ago. . . . Definitely a great value for all of us!"

You never know what items will show up on Freecycle, so be prepared to check the listings regularly. If you're looking for something specific, you can post a "Wanted" message with your desired item for members to see. You can also set up an e-mail alert when a specific item shows up. When you see something you want, reply to the member who posted. And if you're designated the lucky recipient (there may be more than one person interested), arrange to pick it up.

Of course, Freecycle isn't just about getting stuff. It's also a great way to clear out excess stuff. Converting a room in your house into a nursery? Post the items you're getting rid of on your local Freecycle board and get rid of them without even having to load up the car.

- **Craigslist.org.** Your local Craigslist (you'll find a directory at Craigslist.org) is another source of free baby products. You'll find them in the "For Sale" listings under "Free."

     There are some great **local sources**, too. Does your neighborhood organization, church, or other local group have an e-mail list you can join? If so, you may be able to post requests for items or receive notices when members are giving away baby items. Our neighborhood has an e-mail Listserv and parents are constantly posting baby items they're giving away.

- **Gifts.** New babies get gifts, and gifts are free, right? In chapter 3, I'll dish on how to make the most of one of the best sources of free baby items around— the baby shower.

- **Repurpose items you already have.** You may already own more baby gear than you think! By reusing items you may already have when preparing for

baby and setting up the nursery, you can avoid buying things you don't need. For example, your college
backpack could become a sturdy, hands-free diaper
bag. Storage bins and old suitcases can hold baby's
toys. The dresser in your guest room can get a paint
job and become your baby's changing table. Take a
walk around your house before you set foot in a
store. When you think outside the big-box store,
you'll spend less.

- **Promotional freebies and samples.** Earlier in this
chapter I told you how one of the biggest ways advertisers try to get your baby product business is by
getting samples of their wares and coupons into
baby product gift bags (also called welcome kits or
starter kits). As you may have gathered, I'm not a
huge fan of them. But that doesn't mean the samples
and freebies they hold can't be useful. Expect samples of and coupons for diapers, formula, baby bath
products, wipes, diaper ointment, and more.

The gift bag that was the most useful to us was the
freebie hospital diaper bag. If you give birth in a hospital,
chances are they'll give you a diaper bag courtesy of one of
the major formula makers. It will contain formula samples, coupons, and so on. The diaper bag we received was
basic and black—a far cry from the hip designer bags—
but you know what? We used it as an in-the-car bag to
hold extra diapers, wipes, and an extra outfit when my son

was a baby, and we still use it now as a picnic bag. Recycle the advertising, but don't leave your freebie bag behind. It may come in handy!

Repurpose Baby Items When They're Outgrown

Don't be too quick to pass on your baby items after baby has outgrown them, even if you're not planning on using them with your next child. You can help "amortize" the cost of baby items by using them for other purposes. A bottle brush, for example, works well on drinking glasses, while burp cloths make great eco-friendly cleaning cloths. Many a baby food jar has found a second life in the garage holding screws or nuts.

Principle 3: Consider Secondhand Items

Want to save up to 75 percent on baby gear and other items? Buy them secondhand. Babies can outgrow their outfits in as little as a week, and many of the so-cute-you-can't-stand-it outfits received as shower gifts may not get the tags cut off before they're outgrown. That means most of the infants' clothing you'll find on the secondhand market is like new. The same goes for baby gear like bouncers and swings. As a new mom, I was shocked by how quickly my son aged out of our carefully acquired gear. My son was done with his bouncer and swing by about four months.

What would *you* buy used? Each of us has a different comfort level when it comes to accepting secondhand items. Some are okay with items like secondhand bottles, while the very idea gives some folks the heebie-jeebies. Decide which secondhand items you're willing to consider using. A poll of several thousand Baby Cheapskate readers revealed that readers' top items to score used are toys, strollers, play yards, high chairs, and swings.

Me? I have a pretty high tolerance for used items. To me, if an item can be washed with hot water and maybe even a little bleach, it's fair game. We saved big on so many items by finding them at consignment stores, thrift stores, garage sales, and consignment sales. Some of my most prized finds include dozens of baby outfits, a baby gym, a high chair, toys, a wipe warmer, several easy-to-clean bibs, and our white noise machine. We found two baby gates in good condition by the side of the road as someone's trash. And I'll never forget the time I found a $100 French baby outfit with the tags still on it at my local thrift store. Score!

As I noted before, when you're scouting for used items, you'll want to make sure to check items carefully. Make sure they're in good working condition and check to make sure they haven't been recalled.

Where to Find Secondhand Baby Items

- **Garage and yard sales.** Find garage sale listings at Craigslist and on your local newspaper's Web site.
- **Seasonal consignment sales** offered by churches and organizations. Find them at sites like KidsConsign mentSales.com and TheBargainWatcher.com.
- **Consignment stores.** Search for stores near you by Googling "kids consignment store" and the name of your town. Kid to Kid (kidtokid.com) and Once Upon a Child (onceuponachild.com) are national children's resale franchises. Consignment stores are fabulous options if you're not accustomed to buying secondhand items. The condition of gear and toys is screened before they're put on the shelves. You'll pay a bit more than at a thrift store or garage sale, but you can be assured that the items you see are of acceptable quality.
- **Thrift stores.** Find stores near you with a quick Internet search for "thrift store" along with the name of your city. Thrift stores aren't created equal. Selection, quality, and price can vary widely from store to store, so you may need to visit a few before you find one that you like. For the best selection, find out when stores restock the shelves and shop then.
- **Online classifieds.** Craigslist.org and eBayClassi fieds.com list secondhand items available near you.
- **Swap meets.** Swap meets are fabulous ways to ex-

change outgrown baby clothing and gear for new-to-you items. Usually, you drop off your clean, gently used items, they're sorted, and then you get to "shop" with no cash necessary. Plus, these events often feature food, raffles, and other fun activities as well. Sometimes there's an admission charge or membership dues, but not always. Search for swap meets both large and small near you at sites like MeetUp .com. Can't find a swap meet near you? Why not organize your own?

Online Sources for Secondhand Gear

Don't have the time or inclination to get in the car and search for deals on secondhand items? Check out the sites below. They let you buy, swap, or just plain get for free gently used gear, clothing, and more (maternity clothes, too, in many cases) without leaving home. Just be sure to factor shipping and any membership fees into the equation when you're deciding whether you're getting a deal:

- eBay.com
- ThredUp.com
- SwapMamas.com
- ReCrib.com
- SwapBabyGoods.com

Principle 4: If You Can't Get It Free, Get It Cheap

It seems simple, right? Don't buy anything new unless it's on sale. Doing this consistently requires foresight. If you run out of diapers, for example, you don't want to have to run out and pay whatever the asking price is just to avoid having to make your own MacGyver-style out of paper towels, a grocery bag, and some duct tape.

The key to buying items only when they're on sale is doing your research. So shop with a pencil and paper instead of your wallet until you start to get a feel for the going rate of each of the items you're interested in. Now take that retail price and reduce it by 15 percent (or more!). That's your target price.

But wait! Take the savings one step further: Buy at that price *only* if you have a coupon or coupon code. Knowing what coupons are out there will allow you to time your purchases so that you can use a coupon to make sale prices even better. In the next chapter, I'll share my best tips for finding sales and coupons.

Principle 5: Don't Buy It Until You Need It

Why do people buy ahead for baby in the first place? Because it would be pretty inconvenient if you brought home your newborn and didn't have a single diaper, wipe, or swaddling blanket in the house, wouldn't it? We buy ahead to make life easier when the time comes to use the items. It's all too easy to over-prepare and buy things you won't use for months, if at all.

The high chair, for example, is on many stores' "must-have" lists. You really don't need one until your baby is ready to eat solid food (if you ever do; more on that later). For most babies, that's four to six months after birth. So for nearly half a year, that high chair you bought will sit around taking up space.

The same goes for the behemoth of baby items, the ExerSaucer or activity center. Your baby needs to be able to sit up before she can use it, so figure on about four months. That's four months you could spend searching for a free or gently used model to use. Rattles, teethers, baby food makers, Jumperoos, and most baby-proofing equipment are other items you don't need right away, if at all. Avoid shelling out cash for these items until you absolutely have to. Of course, if you can score the items for free, and you have the room to store them, that's a different story.

So take the Boy Scout motto with a grain of salt. Delay purchases until the need arises. There is no cookie-cutter baby gear solution for every baby. Each little person has her own personality. As you get to know your baby, you'll gain a better understanding of what she'll get the most use and enjoyment out of. You can also try out other parents' baby gear—like swings or activity centers—during play-dates to see if it makes your baby coo or cry. Once you know, and once your baby's ready, head to the store (during a sale and with a coupon, of course) and buy. That's the path to smart spending.

You know that saying "nothing tastes as good as skinny feels"? The same applies to spending. The fleeting high of a purchase pales in comparison with how good it feels to have a healthy bank balance. Binge spending can encumber your future with debt and clutter your home. Spending wisely now means being happier and freer to make choices later.

 Takeaway Tips

- Separate your needs from your wants, and minimize expenditures on items you don't need.
- Seek out sources of free baby items.
- Be open to using secondhand items.
- Shop the sales and use coupons.
- Use rebates and other "coupon accompaniments" to deepen discounts.
- Experiment with using store brands rather than national brands.
- Resell baby items to recoup the cost.

Chapter 2

• • •

Building Your Shopping List and Finding Big Discounts

When you discover you have a baby on the way, you become a bit like Dorothy in Oz. You get caught up in a whirlwind, your world gets turned upside down, and you wake up in a strange new one. During the nine-plus months of your journey toward parenthood you walk wide-eyed down an unfamiliar road and meet a bunch of characters. Advertisements and social pressure threaten to make you forget your budget or get carried away.

Think of me as Glenda the good witch. I'm here to help you get those flying monkeys off your back and throw cold water on the notion that you're destined to spend $1,000 a month on your new baby. Your ruby slippers (which look fabulous on you, by the way, despite those swollen ankles) are the saving tools you'll gain from reading this book. Click them together three times—and repeat after me ... "Never pay retail. Never pay retail. Never pay retail."

Do Your Research Before You Shop

In the last chapter, you started down the path to smart spending and discovered the basic principles of saving money on baby items. In chapter 2 we focus on paying the least amount possible for the best possible items. You'll learn how to decide what to buy and how to spot a great price on it.

In order to stay in the black, baby product companies need to get the word out about new products *and* convince you that you can't parent successfully without them. They do that via magazine advertorials and advertising that tells you in a variety of ways that your baby's quality of life will suffer if you don't buy in. But savvy shoppers know that the vast majority of what you see in those glossy pages is completely unnecessary.

Even though the list of essential products for a new baby is quite short, eager parents can't wait to head off to the nearest big-box baby store and load up the shopping cart with Onesies, rattles, and the like. It's exciting, after all! But what's the rush? You have more than nine months to shop. For the first half of your pregnancy, I want you to focus on two tasks:

1. Figure out what's worth buying.
2. Find out how to pay the least amount possible for it.

That's right, moms and dads: Before you shop, and before you register, do some research. Load up on knowledge first; there should be plenty of time for acquisition later.

Figure Out What's Worth Buying

If you can't believe the ads and advertorials, whom *can* you trust to tell you what gear is worth the money? The second part of the book gives specific information about gear, clothing, toys, and more. The advice, tips, and recommendations you'll find there are based on years of research and feedback from thousands of parents who value both savings and quality. Once you've finished reading *The Baby Cheapskate Guide to Bargains*, you should have a good idea of what you'd like to bring into your home for your baby.

If you haven't started making a list of baby gear possibilities, go ahead and jot a few things down, focusing on those basic needs we talked about in the last chapter, of course. A spiral notebook would be perfect for the task.

Or keep your notes online at a site like Evernote.com and you can access them with your smartphone when you shop. It's okay to write down general baby product categories and items now rather than specific products. As you read further in the book, you'll be able to fine-tune your list.

If you want even more feedback after you've read this book, talk to parents—in real life or online—whose opinions you value and whose lifestyle is similar to your own. Ask lots of questions. What are their can't-live-without products? What missteps did they make while shopping for their first child? If you're lucky and live near these wise moms and dads, they may even let you take their baby gear for a test-drive.

The Wisdom of the Crowds

It's really helpful to have the ear of an experienced parent. I'm also a huge believer in the wisdom of the masses. In fact, I tend to trust the collective opinion of a diverse multitude of shoppers over the opinion of just one. Reading multiple reviews or hearing several opinions about a product gives me an overall picture of its advantages and disadvantages. If one parent says that a fitted crib sheet fell apart the first time she washed it, I tend to disregard the review, but if a dozen shoppers say the same thing happened to them, I have to believe that the crib sheet's quality may not be up to snuff. By reading multiple reviews of a product, I also gain insight into aspects of the product that I may not have even considered otherwise, such as whether it runs small or large, and how old a baby is when he gets the most enjoyment or use out of it.

When I want to look over lots of impartial product reviews for free, I head online to one of these sites, which give readers access to product reviews posted by experts and by shoppers across several retailer and consumer Web sites.

Where to Find Unbiased Product Reviews

- **ConsumerSearch.com**: Compares professional product reviews from *Consumer Reports* and the like with actual consumer reviews.
- **Buzzillions.com**: Over 3 million ratings from customers at retailers like Babies"R"Us.com, REI.com, Overstock.com, Zappos.com, eToys .com, Diapers.com, Drugstore.com, and more.
- **Wize.com**: Millions of reviews from consumers as well as professional reviews.

Use personal recommendations and product reviews to evaluate your list of potential baby items. Once you've created a personalized, specific "baby must-have" list, it's time to find out how to pay the least amount possible for the items on it.

There are few things more galling to a bargain shopper than making a purchase, only to find out that the item was marked down another 25 percent the very next day. Timing is crucial when it comes to scoring the best deal. But how do you know if the timing is right? More research, of course!

How Low Will It Go: Tracking Prices

Again, the best way to save is to shop only when items are on sale, and try to use a coupon to make the sale price even better. Not all sales are created equal, however, and to know what kind of deal you're getting, you'll need to find out the going rate for baby items you need. When I say "going rate," I don't mean the manufacturer's suggested retail price (MSRP). Far from it, in fact. I mean the average daily sale price of an item. The two can be quite different, as the examples below will show.

The popular Contours Lite stroller by Kolcraft has a list price of $120. You'd have to be crazy to pay that much, however, since it's regularly available at stores like Walmart, Target, and Amazon.com for around $54. Take it a step further: If you knew that the Contours Lite had spent quite a bit of time on sale for $52, you might wait until the price drops again before you buy.

The ubiquitous Graco Lauren crib is another great example. It lists for about $176, but you can find it for around $150 any day of the week. It often goes on sale for around $140. So you'd want to wait until it hits that price point or below to buy.

All of this may seem mysterious to a novice bargain shopper, but you don't need a crystal ball to track prices. You'll get a good idea of the "real" price of an item by using a price comparison search engine. Google Product Search is my favorite. Go to google.com/products and simply type in the item you're looking for. With a click, you'll see the going rate at a variety of retailers. Note the prices you're seeing for the items on your shopping list.

There are a few other ways to compare prices among retailers. If you're shopping in-store with a smartphone, download an app like Google Shopper. It lets you compare prices at local retailers on the spot. Just scan the bar code of an item or snap a photo and get product search results, including pricing, at various online and local retailers and product reviews.

RedLaser (redlaser.com) and ShopSavvy (shopsavvy .mobi) are two similar apps. While these apps do a good job, they won't find the best price 100 percent of the time, and they probably won't tell you if there's a coupon for the item or store in question.

Reader Tips

Baby Cheapskate readers share their secrets for knowing when they've found a really good deal:

I think an online community, like Baby Cheapskate on Facebook, is invaluable! There are sooo many sites and sales that don't pop up on a Google search. It's nice to put a buzz out to other moms who might know about a site or coupon that you don't! It's also important to know the "average" price so you don't get misled by a "percent off" sale! Many times these sales might say it is 30 percent off, but it ends up being average retail price because the original price is overinflated!

—Amanda

Honestly, if I need an item, I'll just go ahead and get it because I know I will need it sooner or later. Right before I go out, I check all the major stores online that sell it, find coupons, and then go. I don't research for weeks or days trying to find the *best* deal . . . if it is something that costs over $100 and I only save $1 or two, then I am not that worried about it.

—Amber

Take It a Step Further: Finding the "Lowest Price Ever"

Once you know what an item really sells for on any given day, the next step is to find out how low you can expect the price on an item to drop. The goal, naturally, is to buy when the item reaches that price point.

One of the least expensive places to find baby items is

the Internet superstore Amazon.com. Amazon's a bit different than other online retailers in that prices can fluctuate from day to day (or even from hour to hour!) based on prices at other retailers. Amazon attempts to match or beat prices at other stores—especially major stores like Walmart and Target—by lowering prices to compete with sales at those retailers. It's this behavior that makes tracking prices at Amazon so useful, no matter where you plan on buying. Look for an item's price history at Amazon, and in effect you're seeing the price history at a number of popular retailers.

You can learn how high or low baby gear prices at Amazon have gone over time at sites like CamelCamel Camel.com and ZingSale.com. Simply type the name of the item in question into the search bar and you'll see a chart with price fluctuations. Depending on the site, you can view this data by year, past six months, past three months, and so on. You can even set up price watches on specific items and receive an e-mail when the price has dropped to the desired level.

Once you know how low the price has gone, write down your "buy price" for each item on your list and wait for a great sale and/or coupon, if necessary, before you pull the trigger. A smart shopper's buy price will be somewhere between the everyday price of an item and the lowest the item's ever gone. How low *you'll* wait for the price to go depends on your tolerance for risk and your personal savings goals.

At this point in your research it's also a fabulous idea to start checking those secondhand baby item sources to gauge the availability of items there. Visit consignment stores and ask how often they have the items in stock. That way, you'll know whether it's smart to search for the item secondhand, or whether you'll need to buy it new.

MAP, or Why Some Items Don't Go on Sale

Have you ever noticed that some items, like iPods, very rarely go on sale? Others never go on sale for more than, say, 20 percent off. Site-wide coupon codes generally exclude these products, too. That's because the manufacturer has put the kibosh on discounting the item below the manufacturer's minimum advertised price (MAP).

Enacting a MAP policy ensures that prices are standard from retailer to retailer and, in the manufacturer's eyes, both protects the cachet or prestige of the brand and provides a level playing field for all retailers carrying the product. Popular baby products that we see sticking to the MAP price include BOB, Medela, some Baby Jogger strollers, and ERGObaby carriers.

Ways to beat MAP pricing:

Reduce your net price with instant or mail-in rebates.

Take advantage of free gifts or store credits with purchase.

Watch for MAP items at flash-sale or daily deal sites like BabySteals.com or Zulily.com.

Check for closeouts on these items. When manufacturers release a newer model or style of an item, they'll often discount the older models.

Buy secondhand items.

Get the Scoop on Sales,
Clearance, and Closeouts

By now you've created your "must-haves" list and discovered the price you want to pay for each item on it. Congratulations! You've finished with the legwork and it's time to start thinking about making some purchases. You know how much you should spend, so now let's hunt down those low prices. Where do you start?

The old-fashioned way to find out about sales, of course, is to hear about them on the radio, on television commercials, and to scan the store circulars in the newspaper. You can still do all of those with great success, but I find it more efficient to go online. Below I've shared a few of my favorite resources and techniques. Don't grab your car keys or your computer mouse as soon as you finish this chapter, though. In chapter 4, I'll tell you how to cut sale prices even more with coupons and coupon codes.

Starter Steps

Browse the weekly store circulars without forking over a few bucks for the Sunday paper at ShopLocal.com.

Join stores' Facebook pages. Old Navy and Gap, for example, spill the beans about sales at their stores all the time. You can also print coupons for in-store use.

Sign up for e-mail alerts at store Web sites. The Children's Place issues coupons for in-store use this way. So do Carter's and OshKosh B'Gosh. This is also a terrific way to get on the lists to receive Friends and Family sale coupons (seasonal coupons of 25 to 30 percent off). Set up an e-mail address to use when you sign up for offers so that you don't have to share your primary address.

Follow money-saving blogs like BabyCheapskate.com to learn about sales and coupon matchups (how to combine coupons with sales for particular items). At Baby Cheapskate, I publish a weekly Top Diaper Deals post that shows you where to get the best prices on diapers. I also tell you about any coupons that are out there.

Find Out About Sales Before They Happen

Just before the start of each month at BabyCheap skate.com I publish a list of deals and sales that I expect to see that month. My list is based on sales that happened during that month the previous year, and it's generally quite accurate. If you know what discounts to expect, you can time your purchases accordingly. You'll find the monthly deal forecasts at http://bit.ly/BCPredicts.

Predicting Sales

Even with all this information, you may think you have to luck out and stumble upon a terrific sale, but sales aren't as random as you think. I've been tracking major sales at popular baby gear retailers for years, and I can tell you that they generally follow regular patterns. If a store has a 25 percent off Friends and Family sale in June one year, you can expect them to do it again the same week the next year, give or take a few days (Amazon is an exception to this rule; I've found their sales to be highly unpredictable).

Seasonal and store clearance sales follow patterns as well. Stores need to move last season's merchandise out in order to make room for new items. Winter clearance starts just after Christmas and lasts through February, for example. Nonseasonal clearance sales are also predictable at many stores. Target traditionally marks down baby clothes on Mondays and toys on Wednesdays. If you know the schedule, you'll know when to hit the stores. If you're really nice when you ask, store employees may dish about upcoming clearance events.

You can also count on finding closeout deals around the time brands release their newest models. When Britax released their next-generation seats, for instance, the "old models" were cheaper than I had ever seen them. If you hear about a new, "improved" product hitting the market, check your favorite stores for closeout deals on the older version.

What About Warehouse Clubs: Are They Worth It?

Where do warehouse clubs fit in with all of this? Are clubs like Costco, Sam's Club, and BJ's Wholesale Club worth joining? The answer is . . . maybe. You'll need to take a hard look at how you'll use your membership.

Not all clubs are created equal, and one may fit your lifestyle while another may not. Some clubs, for instance, offer unexpected discounts on gas, attraction tickets, tires, eyeglasses, and prescriptions. BJ's Wholesale allows you to use manufacturers' coupons, mails members BJ's coupon books, and offers Internet-printable coupons. Some clubs have huge grocery sections with less-expensive organic products. Some stores allow you to order online and pick up at the warehouse to save time. See what your local warehouse club has to offer.

Warehouse Club Dos and Don'ts

Do: Figure the membership fee into the cost of the items you buy. If the club's membership fee is $45 a year, you'll need to save more than $45 for it to be worth it. Do a little math of your own to see if it really works for you.

Don't: Assume an item is cheaper just because you're in a warehouse club. In my experience, premium brands of diapers and formula aren't a great deal at the clubs. You can generally beat warehouse club pricing when you shop the sales with coupons or shop Amazon Mom. Baby gear tends to be well priced, but expect the selection to be quite slim.

Do: Calculate the price per unit. It's the only way you're going to know if that fifty-gallon drum of baby formula is a good deal. Simply divide the price by the number of ounces, diapers, wipes, and so on, and compare with the price per unit at other retailers.

Do: Stick to your list. As Baby Cheapskate reader Carrie says, "It is so hard to not have impulse . . . purchases there. I have to set a budget and not allow myself to spend any more money than the set amount. I will also not let myself just browse around, but instead get in there for the items I need to get and get out. No sidetracking!" That's not such a big deal at Target, but in this case we're often talking about larger quantities, and thus more money down the drain from impulse buying.

Do: Figure in travel costs. Warehouse clubs aren't on every corner. Do you drive farther to get to one than you would to other stores? Driving isn't free, you know (more on that in a later chapter). You'll need to figure that extra driving cost into the cost of the items.

Do: Check to see if your employer offers discounted warehouse club memberships.

Don't: Buy more of something than you can use before it expires, is outgrown, or becomes obsolete.

Saving with Social Media

Social media, which includes blogs, forums, and sites like Facebook and Twitter, can also help you find out about sales and deals before they happen. In fact, social media is an über-powerful tool for bargain hunting and for parenting in general. Take a look at some of my favorite ways to use social media to save big:

Twitter

Twitter is an efficient way for busy parents to get information they need and to interact with the people behind the baby product brands they depend on. You'll find that most baby product manufacturers and stores have a Twitter presence. Use the Twitter search bar to find and follow them.

The following list of practical ways parents can use Twitter.com will convince you once and for all that Twitter's so much more than a bunch of bored people talking about what they had for lunch.

Find deals, coupons, and more. Start by following @BabyCheapskate for up-to-the-minute deals, coupons, and baby product shopping tips. @Freebies4Mom (the Twitter handle for Freebies4Mom.com) is a great one to follow for freebies. There are lots more great bargain hunters out there, too!

Get news of baby product recalls. Follow @usrecall news, @FDArecalls, @kidsindanger, and/or @safekidsusa and get recall updates and relevant safety information. It's a lot timelier than reading about recalls in next month's parenting magazine.

Let stores and manufacturers know what you think about their products and services, whether good or bad, in 140 characters or less. Tweet with a real, live customer service person to resolve an issue or ask a question. Every time I've done so, I've received a thoughtful, non-copy-and-paste answer. That's so much nicer than sitting on hold for an hour, only to listen to someone read from a script!

Crash the Twitter parties. Twitter parties are hosted by bloggers or by a particular brand of product and are denoted by a hashtag (such as #Graco) at the end of each Tweet. The party host will ask questions. Answer and you could win prizes. Brands often release coupon codes during Twitter parties, too. You can find out about upcoming Twitter parties by "following" the brand of interest.

Facebook

Something else that's really exploded in the past year or two is the publication of coupon codes on retailers' Facebook pages. "Like" the pages of your favorite retailers and watch your Facebook stream for announcements of coupon codes and special sales. You can also visit the retailers' pages to ask questions about sales and get customer feedback about the stores from other fans. Some retailers even offer customer service via their Facebook pages.

Reader Tips

I find that Facebook is the best way to be alerted to deals, coupons, and sales since I don't check my e-mail but a few times a day and Facebook is perpetually updating. Plus I can instantly see others' reviews and questions about the topic.

—Erasmia

I follow my favorite brands on Facebook and check their pages for limited-time specials and deals!

—Sarah

Couponing Forums

Become a member of deal forums like SlickDeals.net, HotCouponWorld.com, and AFullCup.com. There are forum sections dedicated to the most popular stores, and members (and even anonymous store employees) dish about upcoming sale and clearance events. These sites often feature scans of store circulars before they're released in the paper—great for planning ahead.

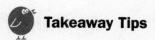 **Takeaway Tips**

- Read product reviews and talk to experienced parents to find out what's worth buying.

- Track prices on items to find out what price you should pay.
- Use Web sites and apps to compare prices between stores.
- Try to shop only when an item's on sale.
- Try to use a coupon or coupon code each time you shop.
- Always compare prices per unit when buying in bulk to ensure that you're getting a good deal.
- "Like" Facebook pages and "Follow" the Twitter accounts of brands you like to get coupons and find out about sales.
- Check "deal" blogs and Web sites for sale announcements and coupon codes. Some also offer coupon-trading forums.

Chapter 3

Creating the Registry: From Woombies to Onesies

For me, creating my baby registry was one of the most fun things about being pregnant, just like creating my bridal registry was one of the best things about planning my wedding. Walking the aisles and scanning items just because they were adorable or looked vaguely useful was pure girly bliss. Creating a registry felt like a shopping spree with the benefit of not having to stand in line and fork over money at checkout. Instead, everything would be wrapped and presented to me at my shower or after the baby was born.

Sure, registering was a ton of fun, but because I lacked a plan, I missed out on some major baby savings and I embarked on my journey of parenthood without a lot of the things I actually needed. That's why I'm here to say step away from the scanner, sister. Let's talk first.

I realize there may be a few of you out there who don't plan on registering at all (What?!). Maybe you think it's cheesy, or you don't plan on having a baby shower. While you certainly don't *have* to register at all, I recommend it. Registries and baby showers can help parents cut the cost of preparing for baby dramatically—if you know how to do it right. With a little—you guessed it—strategizing, your registry can be a real money-saving tool.

Where Will You Register?

Where you register depends, in part, on the generous folks who you think will be buying from your registry. Do most of them live nearby, or will they be shipping the goodies to you? If you have lots of out-of-town family and friends, choosing a store with a free shipping deal or flat-rate shipping (good for larger items) is a good idea.

Keep in mind that less technologically inclined folks may not feel comfortable buying online. It's good to have a brick-and-mortar option. And it's perfectly acceptable to create a registry at more than one store.

It's also important to consider the store's return policy. Most of us end up returning *something*, and you want to avoid hassles. Be sure to keep track of all your gift receipts.

Another cool thing about registering at a brick-and-mortar store is that most allow you to purchase leftover items on your registry at a discount. Most of the time it's

10 percent off. Find out about the store's registry completion program before you sign up. Of course, 10 percent off isn't really anything to shout about, so if you're buying leftover items off your registry, be sure to do a price comp first to make sure you're getting the best deal you can.

The 4 Most Popular Places to Register

- **Babies"R"Us** (www.babiesrus.com/registry). Advantages: In-store and online options (return gifts to either). Disadvantages: Shipping costs, strict return policy.
- **Buy Buy Baby** (www.buybuybaby.com). Advantages: In-store and online options (return gifts to either), reputation for good customer service.
- **Target** (www.target.com/registry/baby/portal). Advantages: In-store and online options (return gifts to either). Disadvantages: Gift receipts or "gift purchase log" required for return.
- **Amazon.com** (www.amazon.com/gp/baby/homepage). Advantages: Free shipping on most items at $25. Huge selection. Good prices. Disadvantages: Online only. You'll have to ship items back to Amazon to return them.

What About Universal Registries?

Wouldn't it be nice if you didn't have to choose one store to register with? What if you could add items from any store out there onto one list? Well, you can! With universal registries, you drag an "Add to Registry" button to your Internet browser's toolbar. Then, whenever you see something online that you want to add to your registry, just click. You can even register for cool handmade items from sites like Etsy.com with a universal registry.

Gift givers browse your registry at the universal registry Web site, and are directed to the Web site of the store that's actually selling the item when they're ready to buy. Returns are also handled by the Web site or store that sells the item. One drawback about universal registries is that friends and family members who aren't comfortable using the Internet for shopping may have a harder time understanding the idea of and figuring out how to use a universal registry than they would a regular online registry.

Baby Cheapskate readers are big fans of Amazon .com's Universal Registry (www.amazon.com/gp/registry/universal). Because Amazon is so popular, many users are already comfortable with the interface. That's a plus. Amazon also lets you prioritize items on your registry. Another plus!

MyRegistry.com is another popular choice. It offers an app for the iPhone or Android that lets you add items to your registry while shopping in-store by scanning the item's bar code with your phone. With MyRegistry.com, you can also register for "cash gifts," although the site charges the giver a small fee ($4 to $7 currently, depending on the amount of the gift).

Be Smart: Register for the Essentials

My very best tip for creating a registry is to focus on the items on the "need" list you created based on the tips in the last chapter. Especially important to include on your registry are items that you don't think you'll be getting for free or purchasing secondhand. That includes things like car seats, along with diapers, wipes, and other not-so-glamorous items. A case (or five) of diapers may not have the same "Awwwwww" factor as a tiny pink dress, but you'll be glad later to have the diapers.

By registering for essentials, you won't be stuck handing over money for items you can't live without while you have a closetful of adorable newborn clothes that will be outgrown in two weeks and rattles that your baby may or may not ever give a shake about. Skip the *War and Peace*–sized registry checklists offered by retailers. They're packed with nonessentials.

Reader Tip

Take a friend who's had a baby in the last two years, she can shed wonderful info on the current must-have trends and items that were better left on the shelf.

—Jess

10 Baby "Needs" Worth Registering For

- Crib
- Crib mattress
- Crib bedding
- Diapers (cloth or disposable)/wipes
- Formula (if you plan to use it)
- Breast pump
- Bottles
- Disposable or washable breast pads
- Car seat
- Baby thermometer

If you're not into scouting for secondhand items, consider adding some of these popular big-ticket extras, like strollers, to your registry so that you won't have to pay for them out of pocket later. Friends and family can go in together on items that would be too expensive otherwise. We'll talk about these big-ticket extras—cribs, strollers, and so on—in more detail later in the book.

10 Popular Extras Worth Registering For

- Baby carrier
- Stroller
- Portable play yard
- Bouncer
- Swing
- Diaper bag
- Diaper pail
- Baby monitor
- Nursing cover
- Swaddling blankets or swaddling gowns

If (and *only* if) you have the room to store them, it's also helpful to register for things you'll need a few months down the road, like a high chair. If you're short on space, consider adding gift cards to your registry so that you can pick up gear and other items as your baby reaches the age where she can use them.

Popular Extras for Later On

- High chair
- Baby food storage jars
- Umbrella stroller
- Baby-proofing items

Registry items don't always have to come from a store. Drop a few hints about these to whoever's hosting your shower and you'll be glad you did:

Other Really Cool Things to "Register" For

- Gift cards to photo print and gift Web sites
- Homemade meals for the freezer
- Gift certificates for something to make a new mom feel pampered (manicure, haircut, and so on)
- Gift certificate for an hour of babysitting

You may have noticed that there's not a stitch of baby clothing on the lists. Here are two reasons why: First, baby clothing is super-easy to find secondhand; second, people will buy it for you anyway. They won't be able to resist. The same goes for rattles and teethers. In part 2 of this book, we'll go over layettes, and talk about what you'll want to make sure you have by the time the baby arrives.

Reader Tips

Don't be afraid to register for things that are "too expensive." All my friends told me to register for everything I need, no matter the price, because people will buy what they want to buy. To think I would have missed out on my stroller.

—Rachel

Have mom friends looking over your registry. I did that and got a lot of "Oh, I have one of those that my kids are no longer using. Do you want it?" I got a Boppy, a Bumbo, and a few other things that way.

—Laura

Register for neutral-color big-ticket items. Odds are you will have more kids and you will want them to work for both genders. Also don't wash and open items you registered for until you know you are going to use them. You can't return items if they are washed or out of the box.

—Jackie

Consider the seasons when registering. Your store may have summer clothing and bedding out when you register for your winter baby. You want to make sure you are ready for each season!

—Christina

How Many Items Should You Put on Your Registry?

How many items you put on your registry depends on how many people you think you'll have buying from it. If you have too many, you may not get what you need the most. On the other hand, if you have too few, your generous friends will improvise, for better or worse. *(continued)*

As a rule of thumb, approximate the number of people you think will be shopping from your registry and add 20 percent. Be sure you have that many items on your list. That way, you'll focus on the things you need, or really, really want, and still give folks a few gift-giving options.

Registries for Multiples

Expecting twins, triplets, or other multiples? Luckily, you don't need to register for two (or more) of everything since babies can share or use items at alternate times. You *will* need a shocking number of diapers and wipes, however. You may want to sit down for this statistic: Parents of twins, for example, will change five thousand to seven thousand diapers in one year. So whether you choose cloth or disposable diapers, make sure they're on your registry. Another thing you'll definitely need two or more of is infant car seats. Put them on your registry, too.

While having multiples *is* more expensive than having singletons, there are some special discounts out there for you that will take a little of the sting out of the price tag. Some stores, like Babies"R"Us, offer discounts and freebies for parents (or soon-to-be parents) of multiples. Some brands, like Huggies, Pampers, Medela, and the First Years, offer discounts on their gear to parents of multiples as well. You may need some kind of proof that you have multiples to get the discounts. Copies of your kids' birth certificates will generally do the trick.

If you don't know any other parents of multiples, be sure to join a multiples group, either local or online. Experienced parents can offer advice about what else you'll need two (or more) of and how to find the best values. They can also be a great source of "I've been there" support when the going gets rough. You can find local multiples groups with a quick Internet search for "multiples group" or "twins group." Mothers of Multiples (MOM) groups are located in many cities. You'll find a directory of local clubs at the National Organization of Mothers of Twins Clubs Web site (www.nomotc.org).

Twins magazine is a great source of resources for parents of twins (www.twinsmagazine.com). Triplet Connection (www.tripletconnection.org) has an active (and free) message board where you can connect with other parents. MOST (Mothers of SuperTwins) is another online resource to check out (www.mostonline.org).

Reader Tips

Write to as many baby brands as you can think of, including the diaper companies. Include a copy of the birth certificates and request any multiple program they might have. I'm doing this now for my twins, many companies are willing to help support you!

—Laine

We went with booster seats instead of traditional high chairs to save space. And if I had it to do again I'd get travel swings instead of full-size swings, again to save space.

—Michelle

We bought quite a few items used in excellent condition from other families of multiples. For example, we paid $25 for our Jumperoo and $25 for an ExerSaucer. Our Bumbos were only $10 each and they look brand-new. We were able to put the money we saved toward diapers, cribs, car seats, and so on.

—Jennie

It's Raining Freebies: Baby Showers

While some moms-to-be can't wait for their first baby shower, others throw up a little in their mouths when they think about these pink- or blue-festooned occasions. Psst. You latter types, lean a little closer to this page. I've got a little message for you:

Don't be a stick-in-the-mud! Even if you're not the "baby shower type," have a baby shower (or two!). They don't have to be traditional; help your host design a party that's more *you*. As the name suggests, the purpose of a baby shower is to shower you with baby gear. Now's not the time to get bashful about getting gifts. You're going to need this stuff, after all.

Here are a few ideas that will help you get the most out of your baby shower(s):

Don't Be Afraid to Break the Rules

It used to be gauche for family members to throw you a shower, but it's pretty common today. If a friend doesn't offer to host a shower for you, go ahead and let Aunt Sue do it.

It's also perfectly acceptable to include dads-to-be in the fun. After all, they're becoming parents, too! I love the idea of including your guy. It just seems more modern to me, and suggests that raising a baby is something that both parents do, rather than just Mom. Of course, the guys may not go for those traditional baby shower games. Plan on keeping it casual. A barbecue, perhaps?

When should you have your shower? Most baby showers take place about six weeks before the due date, but don't feel bound to tradition. You can have it earlier or later than that. We actually waited until after the baby was born to have our shower. My son was a couple months old, and by then we had a really good idea of what we needed for a newborn. Waiting to have the shower is an especially useful idea if you're keeping the baby's gender secret, or waiting until birth to find out. Guests will know exactly who the little human is that their gift is for. Plus, if you wait to have your shower, guests arriving from out of town also get the chance to see the new baby.

My Favorite Baby Shower Ideas

- **Stock up on diapers.** I love the idea of a diaper raffle. Guests bring a pack of diapers (or a cloth diaper) and exchange it for a raffle ticket. At the end of the shower, the hostess chooses the winning ticket, and the winner gets a gift. As Baby Cheapskate reader Jen says, "For the price of a few gift cards, you will have an abundance of diapers!"

- **Build a board book library.** Have guests bring a beloved board book to the shower. Babies love to hear Mom's or Dad's voice, and they'll love to sit with you and "read" long before they can hold the book themselves. Or why not have guests bring their favorite parenting book in lieu of a gift?

- **Have a "handmade" shower.** Maybe you're a minimalist mama who doesn't want to bring too much baby stuff into the house. Or maybe you're the creative type yourself. Create meaningful memories by having guests bring handmade items rather than shop from a registry. From fun mobiles to hand-painted bodysuits to tasty treats the mom-to-be can pop into the freezer, everybody's sure to come up with something fabulous.

- **Go secondhand.** A friend of mine had a "secondhand" baby shower. Her guests brought gently used baby gear, clothing, and other items. I love this idea. You'll get the gear you need, your guests will pay less, and it's good for the planet, too. Some consignment stores even have registries. Guests who aren't up for secondhand shopping could bring gift cards or diapers.

After the Shower Ends

Once the gifts have all been carted home, what do you do? (Besides write thank-you notes, of course.) It's time to get organized! Take stock of your registry. Find out what you still *need* for the baby, when you need it by, and how you might get it for less.

When it comes to clothing, I recommend leaving tags on and waiting before you wash. That way, you'll be able to return or exchange what doesn't get worn. The same goes for baby gear that you won't need right away: Leave it in the box. Tape gift receipts to boxes so they'll be easy to find.

And don't worry about offending anyone by returning items that don't work for you. As Baby Cheapskate reader Danae reminds us, "The whole point of the registry is to get something you need/want for baby."

Procrastination Pays Off

Wait as late as you possibly can (without panicking) before buying the remainder of what you need. Remember, in many cases you can wait until *after* the baby is born to buy unfulfilled registry items.

 ## Takeaway Tips

- Register for essentials and big-ticket items.
- Consider registering for diapers and wipes.
- Think about whether potential gift givers will be comfortable with online registries when deciding where to register.
- Expecting multiples? Consult other parents of multiples to pinpoint your registry needs.
- Leave tags on gifts and wait before you wash in case you need to return something later.

Chapter 4

• • •

Saving Big with Coupons

 If you saw a dollar lying on the sidewalk, would you pick it up? How about a quarter? A nickel? A penny?

Coupons are like found money to the savvy shopper. They're valuable tools in every parent's baby-savings tool kit. Attitudes toward couponing vary, however. Some people—the ones you don't want to get stuck behind in the checkout line—view couponing as a competitive sport. They keep a huge coupon binder, trade for coupons online, buy coupons from coupon-clipping services, and know just how to match up coupons with sales to save the most.

Others of us are content to be casual couponers. We're happy to stoop for a dollar or two, but we're not as eager to scoop up small change from the sidewalk. We'll use high-value coupons whenever we can, but we like the couponing process to be quick and easy. The amount of effort you're willing to invest in couponing depends on your budget, your lifestyle, and a handful of other factors.

This chapter follows up on the fourth principle of savings: "If you can't get it free, get it cheap." You know how to find sales, and now you'll discover how to save even more by combining those sales with coupons. And don't think I'm going to show you how to coupon like those crazies on TLC's *Extreme Couponing* show, either. Instead, I'll help you discover some quick, easy, and *sane* ways to use coupons to save serious money on baby stuff—20 percent or more. Whether you've got five minutes or five hours to devote to searching for and using coupons, this chapter will convince you that couponing is worth it. Like change on the sidewalk, the savings, after all, are there for the taking.

Couponing Basics for the Absolute Beginner

Couponing can seem a little mysterious to those who have never tried it, but it's really a cinch. If you're brand-new to the Q, here are a few basic couponing concepts:

- There are two types of coupons: manufacturer's coupons and store coupons. The former is issued by— you guessed it—the manufacturer, while the other is issued by the retailer and can only be used there. The top of the coupon should tell you which type you have. Great news: You may be able to use a manufacturer's coupon *with* a store coupon for extra savings.

- Read the coupon carefully for restrictions. Note the size of the package you'll need to buy, the quantity of items you'll need to buy, and the date the coupon expires.
- You can generally use one manufacturer's coupon per item. If you buy more than one, you can generally use more than one coupon.
- Hand your coupons to the cashier after your items have been rung up.
- When it comes to a store's coupon policy, the store manager has the final say.
- Keep your coupons organized. Coupons have expiration dates, and if you forget to use a coupon before it expires, it's worthless. Find an organizational system that works for you. I find it helpful to sort coupons by categories (baby, grocery, health and beauty, and so on) and put coupons expiring first in the front. When I make my shopping list, I put a "C" next to the items I have coupons for.
- Store-brand products may still cost you less even if you have a coupon. Do a quick price-per-unit check to see if that's the case before you buy a name-brand item with a coupon.

Reader Tips

I like sorting my coupons in an index card file box that
fits in my diaper bag/large purse versus a large binder.
They are alphabetical by brand name!

—Jennifer

Keep coupons in a zip-up binder that would usually be
used for baseball cards. That way there are individual
slots for each coupon and you can add extra plastic
sleeves as needed. I try to keep my binder in the car at
all times, because . . . you will never know when you will
come across a fabulous deal. Also . . . keep out of reach
of children. Nothing is worse than finding your coupons
all over the floor in the hands of a two-year-old!

—Heather

A good deal is not always a good deal. It is important to
know your prices and wait to use coupons until the item
is at a rock-bottom (or pretty close to it) price. $.50 off
full price is not saving the most you can on a product.

—Carrie

10 Commonly Used Couponing Terms

Visit a Web site, blog, or forum devoted to couponing and
you're sure to see terminology that you may not know the
meaning of. Couponing beginners can be intimidated by
the vocabulary and acronyms thrown about by experi-

enced couponers. Here's a list of terms you'll hear used by coupon enthusiasts. Learn them and coupons will become your BFF ASAP!

- YMMV: Your mileage may vary (in other words, "you may not get the same deal I did")
- AR: After rebate
- BOGO: Buy one get one
- OOP: Out-of-pocket expense
- OYNO: On your next order
- WYB: When you buy
- Stacking: Using more than one coupon at a time
- Peelie: Coupons found attached to the outside of a product
- Tear pad: Tear-off pads of coupons found on store shelves
- Catalina: A machine found in stores (usually attached to shelves) that spits out coupons

On the Hunt: The Best Coupon Sources

To marketers, coupons are promotional tools geared at getting you to try a new product or store. The idea is that if you like the product or store, you'll buy it again or shop there again regardless of whether you have a coupon. Of course, the goal of every bargain shopper is to make sure she *does* have that magic little scrap of paper, especially when it comes to baby consumables like disposable diapers, wipes, formula, and toiletries. So where do you get them? Read on.

Baby Coupon Sign-Ups

Want a no-fuss way to get coupons for consumable baby products? Have them delivered to your mailbox. Here's a gimmick-free, spam-free list of sites where you can sign up to receive baby-related coupons and samples by mail or e-mail:

Coupons for Disposable Diapers and Wipes
- Pampers: www.pampers.com/en_US/signup
- Huggies: www.huggies.com/en-US/register
- Seventh Generation: www.seventhgeneration.com/coupons

Coupons for Formula
- Enfamil Family Beginnings: www.enfamil.com
- Similac Strong Moms: www.similac.com
- GoodStart: www.gerber.com/login/register.aspx

Coupons for Baby Food
- Gerber: www.gerber.com/login/register.aspx
- Beech-Nut: www.beechnut.com/Special%20Offers/
- Nature's Goodness (Del Monte): www.naturesgoodness.com

- HappyBaby: www.happybabyfood.com/community/
  79/126-sign-in
- Sprout: www.sproutbabyfood.com

Baby Clubs

Check to see if your favorite grocery and department stores have baby clubs. These free clubs are useful because often you can combine the store coupons they send you with manufacturers' coupons. With some programs, you accumulate rewards for spending on baby stuff. Here are a few:

- Winn-Dixie Baby Club: www.winndixie.com/
  Reward_Card/Baby_Club_Program.asp
- Publix Baby Club: www.publix.com/clubs/baby/
  Subscribe.do
- ShopRite Baby Bucks: www.shoprite.com/Baby
  Bucks.aspx
- Save-A-Lot Being Well Baby Club: www.save-a-lot
  .com/ads-promotions/promotions/being-well-baby
- Price Chopper Baby Club: www2.pricechopper.com/
  babyclub/index.shtml

You can also get coupons for signing up for e-mail and birthday clubs at kiddie clothing retailers like The Children's Place or Crazy8. Target also sends out lots of store coupons by mail.

Newspaper Coupon Inserts

Another reliable place to find coupons for disposable diapers, wipes, baby food, and the like is in the SmartSource, Valassis (RedPlum), and brandSAVER coupon inserts you'll find in your local newspaper. They're usually in Sunday's paper, but in some places they're in one of the weekday editions.

Coupons for disposable diapers follow a predictable schedule. Huggies and Pampers coupons are released monthly in the newspaper circulars. The Huggies coupons are in the SmartSource circular, and the Pampers coupons come in Procter & Gamble's brandSAVER insert.

Reader Tip

I also make a habit of checking the Web sites of products I prefer to find coupons when I need one. Some sites will allow you to print a new coupon every month. Use coupons to stock up when nonperishables are clearanced or priced at or near their lowest prices.

—Kristy

Printable Coupons

You can also print manufacturers' coupons online for in-store use at sites like Coupons.com and SmartSource.com. Most of these sites let you print each coupon twice.

Check brands' Web sites for printable coupons, free samples, and other offers as well. You can print coupons for Earth's Best baby food, for example, at www.earths best.com. Some stores, like Target, Kroger, and CVS, offer printable coupons or eCoupons at their Web sites.

What About Organics?

A common criticism about couponing is that coupons are easy to find for processed food but few and far between when it comes to natural and organic items. It's true that if you prefer organic or natural products, which tend to be pricier than processed foods, you may have a harder time finding coupons, but that doesn't mean they're not out there. Here are four places to look:

- Check the Web sites and Facebook pages of your favorite eco-friendly brands for printable coupons.
- While you're at these Web sites and Facebook pages, see if there's a mailing list or newsletter you can sign up to receive.
- The Web site MamboSprouts.com is a great place to check for printable coupons for organic products, especially milk and cereals.
- Stores that sell organic products, like Whole Foods, often have printable coupons on their Web sites as well.

Decoding Coupon Codes

Coupon codes, for any uninitiated shoppers among you, are how the Internet does discounts. Whereas paper coupons allow you to save on consumable products like diapers and wipes, coupon codes let you cut costs by up to 50 percent or so on non-consumables, like baby gear and clothing. They're a breeze to use, too. Just type the coupon code into the designated spot at checkout and save. Most, though not all, shopping sites release coupon codes on a fairly regular basis. Most codes are for 10 to 50 percent off your purchase or off a particular item. There are several ways to find coupon codes online:

- Follow your favorite stores and brands on Twitter and watch your Twitter stream for codes.
- "Like" your favorite stores' and brands' Facebook pages and watch for special coupon codes and promotions.
- Check coupon code aggregating sites like RetailMe Not.com for codes.
- Keep up with deal blogs that post coupon codes.

$ QUICK AND EASY SAVINGS $

My favorite way to scout for coupon codes is simply to Google the name of the site plus "coupon code" and then sort the results chronologically. That should be enough to pull up any current codes.

Reader Tip

By following a few key bloggers, you'll learn all the tricks to saving big, without doing any of the work. The bloggers can tell you what the sales are and where to find the coupons to match up. It doesn't get any easier than that!

—Rebeca

Check In and Check Out: Mobile Coupons

Mobile coupons are the newest kid on the couponing block. Mobile coupons are either text messages sent to your cell phone or apps that you download to your smartphone. To use them, simply show the coupon or text message to the cashier. You can sign up to receive mobile coupons at retailers' Web sites (like Target.com) and/or check a mobile coupon aggregator like 8coupons.com or mobile coupons.com.

Some mobile couponing sites, like the ones listed below, are location-based. They use your phone's GPS to send you coupons when you arrive at or check in at a store:

- Cellfire.com (also offers printable coupons)
- Zavers.com
- Foursquare.com (get coupons delivered to your smartphone when you "check in" at a store that offers them)
- CouponSherpa.com
- GetYowza.com (smartphone app–based)
- GroceryIQ.com (integrated coupons and grocery lists)

TAKE IT A STEP FURTHER: CALLING FOR COUPONS Really want a coupon? Readers who call customer service often end up with coupons whether they're sharing how much they like a product, expressing concern over some aspect of it, or just plain asking for coupons. It never hurts to try!

Loyalty Cards, Rebates, and Vouchers: Three More Cost Cutters

While the following aren't technically coupons, no discussion of couponing is complete without these ways to save:

Store Loyalty Cards and Programs

Stores use your store loyalty card to track your spending habits and offer you deals that they think will bring you into the store. When you sign up for loyalty programs, you'll usually be required to give the store your e-mail address, telephone number, and address. As I mentioned before, I recommend setting up an e-mail address just for sign-ups and offers so that you keep your primary e-mail address spam-free.

In exchange for surrendering some of your shopping privacy, you can expect special coupons or savings on your purchases. With some programs, you accumulate points toward a reward or cash back. Opt out of loyalty programs at some stores, like Kroger, CVS, and Rite Aid, and you won't get the advertised sale price.

Get Cash Back with Rebates

Mail-in rebates allow you to save a little extra on your net purchase. They're one way stores get around minimum advertised prices in order to beat the competition and win your business.

Let's say you buy a breast pump whose manufacturer is offering a $50 rebate. To get your rebate, you'll need a rebate form (most often found on the packaging, near the item on the shelves, at the cash register, or online) and your receipt. You'll often need to send in the UPC code(s) from the package(s) as well. There may be other hoops to jump through, too, right down to the color ink you use on the form. Be sure to read the fine print. And be sure you send everything in on time.

The problem with mail-in rebates is that sometimes you never get what you have coming to you. Try to call and follow up and you'll probably be given the telephone equivalent of a blank stare. That's why I consider mail-in rebate savings a lagniappe, or a little something extra rather than a basic way to save. The cash back is great if you get it, but don't make it essential to the deal.

Be sure to make legible copies of everything you send in for the rebate so that you have a record. If you don't receive your rebate, file a complaint with the Federal Trade Commission. The FTC also advises filing a complaint with your state's attorney general or the local Better Business Bureau.

Instant rebates, on the other hand, are less of a hassle since they pay you back immediately. Online, an instant rebate works just like a coupon code. In-store, it's an amount that will be subtracted from your purchase price, like a manufacturer's or store coupon.

You can find rebates of both types with an Internet search for the name of the product or brand plus "rebate." Sort your results so that the most recent postings come up first. You can also find lists of current rebates at couponing Web sites. Look for forum topics like "rebates," "refunds," or "mail-in offers." These forums are great for picking up even more tips on saving with rebates.

Vouchers from Groupon and the Other Daily Deal Sites

You can't talk about coupons without talking about sites like Groupon.com, LivingSocial.com, Eversave.com, and the like. Over the past couple of years dozens of these sites have sprung up, offering vouchers for savings of 30 to 80 percent for local and online stores and services.

These sites owe their phenomenal success to the lure of the limited-time-only deal. We buy in because we're afraid we'll miss out if we don't. Add in the allure of getting free credits for referrals, and you've got a recipe that's pretty hard to resist.

Saving 50 percent at a local or online store is terrific as long as you're not signing up to spend unnecessarily. A deal's not a deal if you're suckered into spending on something you really don't need. If you're buying a voucher to use at a Web site, be sure to check out the site before you buy. Make sure it's a site worth buying from.

**4 Things to Remember
When Buying from Daily Deal Sites**

- Are you using the voucher to buy something you would have bought anyway?
- Can you use the voucher by the expiration date?
- What kind of shipping charge will you pay?
- Are there any restrictions about what you can buy or when you can use the voucher?

3 Ways to Take
Couponing Even Further

Double and Triple Coupons

Baby Cheapskate reader Lizzy only shops at grocery stores that double or triple her coupons. That way, she says, she gets more bang for her buck. Some stores double coupons up to a certain amount—say, $.50 or $1—every day, while others have special double coupon events. It's easy to see how double coupons can really amp up your savings. Be sure to check the writing on the coupon to avoid disappointment at checkout. Some say "Do Not Double."

Coupon-trading Groups

Coupon-trading groups are usually e-mail Listservs that allow you to swap, give away, and pick up coupons. Baby Cheapskate has a baby coupon-trading group with more than three thousand members (http://bit.ly/BCCoupon Traders). You can find other trading groups with a quick Internet search.

Maximize Your Savings with Coupons from a Clipping Service

If there's an irresistible deal and you don't have the coupons you need, you can usually get them from a coupon-clipping service. I like CouponClippers.com. An Internet search for "coupon clipping service" will pull up others. Clipping services allow you to have multiples of the same coupons mailed to you. By law, the coupons are free, but you'll pay a handling fee and postage. There's often a minimum order, so go in with another parent if you can. Be sure to factor in the coupons' service charge and shipping to be sure you'll still be getting a deal.

Where to Learn More About Couponing

If you want to learn even more about coupons and how to use them, become a regular at one of several forums devoted to couponing. HotCouponWorld.com, AFullCup

.com, and WeUseCoupons.com are three of my favorites. Each of these popular forums has topics just for newbies, so start there. Couponing forums are online communities with their own quirky rules, so read the forum guidelines before you post.

Takeaway Tips

- Sign up to receive coupons for consumable baby products by mail.
- Get coupons and freebies by joining stores' baby clubs.
- Check newspaper coupon inserts for diaper, wipe, formula, and bath product coupons.
- Search the Internet for printable coupons.
- Coupons for organic products are harder to find, but they're out there.
- Don't buy anything online without checking for a coupon code first.
- Smartphones offer new access to coupons via location-based apps.
- Follow rebate rules and guidelines carefully to increase your chances of getting cash back.
- Avoid impulse purchases when it comes to daily deals.

PART TWO

. . . .

Life's Little Necessities

Chapter 5

• • •

Setting Up the Nursery: Cool Cribs and More

According to *Time* magazine, Victoria Beckham spent $240,000 on a bunny-themed nursery for her latest baby. Wow, talk about the posh life! Many people's houses don't cost that much.

Ah, the nursery. No other room in the house gets so much attention and so little conscious use by the resident it's created for. Let's be honest: Nursery design is for parents, not babies. Small babies don't spend much time in their rooms. They sleep in bouncers, swings, carriers, Pack 'n Plays, and anywhere else they choose. They couldn't care less what it looks like.

True, the Beckhams reportedly spent about 93 percent more than the average family spends on their nursery ($1,600), but the average family still spends way more than it needs to.

Setting up the nursery is one of the most fun parts of

preparing for baby, but how can new parents avoid over-spending? We spent around $500 outfitting my son's nursery. Reusing items we already had, refurbishing a few secondhand pieces, and making our own art helped us cut costs.

In this chapter, I'll clue you in on what you do and don't need, and I'll tell you about some cool DIY ideas. As you read, keep the savings principles from part 1 of this book firmly planted in your mind. First, some basics.

5 Basic Ideas for Nursery Planning

- A nursery is not a need.
- Design a nursery that will grow with your child.
- Repurpose what you already have.
- KISS: Keep it simple. A lot of the stuff the baby product industry wants you to buy for the nursery is pretty useless. Some of it's even a danger to your child (more about that later).
- Consider your decor in the rest of your home when designing your nursery.

I know what you're thinking: What the heck do I mean saying that a nursery is not a need? While your baby needs shelter and a safe place to sleep, she does not require a whole room's worth of it. Of course, it's nice to have a dedicated place to keep all your baby items and gear, but if you're short on space, there's no reason to think you need to call the movers right away. Many a parent has converted an alcove, walk-in closet, or corner of the room into a makeshift nursery. Turn to Ohdeedoh.com's "Smaller Cooler Nursery" posts for dozens of design ideas and a whole heap of inspiration.

7 Space-maximizing Tips for a Mini Nursery

Whether your nursery is tiny or you're trying to fit more than one kid into an average-sized room, these tips will help you maximize your space:

- **Skip the changing table.** Affix a changing pad to a small dresser. Many parents just use a changing pad wherever it's convenient and safe—the bed, the floor, wherever.
- **Think small and skinny.** Choose smaller furniture. A mini crib saves space. There are even cribs made to fit in the corner if that's the only spot you have. Think skinny with your storage. A tall, narrow dresser won't take up as much space as a low, wide one.
- **Use the walls.** Hang shelves instead of using a bookshelf to save space.
- **Think high and low for storage.** Slide a rolling bin under a crib (or choose a crib with a shelf under-

neath). Even cute vintage suitcases would work. Create storage all the way up to the ceiling with shelving.

- **Max out your closet space.** Use the space under those tiny clothes hanging in the closet for shelving or drawers. Install a second overhead shelf in the closet above the one that's already there for items you don't need to access frequently (next season's wardrobe, for example). A hanging shoe rack on the back of the closet door (I like the ones with clear plastic pockets) can hold everything from socks to extra diaper cream.
- **Hang it.** Install a row of hooks on the back of the closet door and/or bedroom door, and use them to store clothing, diaper bags, and so on.

What About Cosleeping?

While having your baby sleep in the bed with you can allow you to skip the bulky crib, cosleeping is not recommended by the American Academy of Pediatrics or the U.S. Consumer Product Safety Commission. For that reason, I won't be offering options for cosleeping in this book. Despite the cautionary guidelines, some parents still choose to cosleep. If it interests you, head to sites like Ask DrSears.com to learn more about safer cosleeping.

Designing the Nursery: Inspiration and Advice

What will your baby's nursery look like? Some parents have known the answer to this question for years, while others have no idea. If you're in the latter group, you'll find hundreds of gorgeous nursery decor ideas at Ohdeedoh .com and ProjectNursery.com.

My best advice? Choose a theme or color scheme that will grow with your child. Design for a five-year-old, rather than a young baby, to avoid having to repaint or redesign when your pre-K kid says his room is too baby-ish. You may have had your heart set on vintage Winnie-the-Pooh, but sticking with a simpler, more generic decor scheme can be easier on the budget and just as fun. If you're not confined to a quirky palette, you'll find it easier to locate matching bedding and accessories at reasonable prices. Plus, if you choose a color scheme that blends with the colors you already have in your "grown-up" decor, you'll be able to mix and match pieces you already have around your home.

$ QUICK AND EASY SAVINGS: REPURPOSE WHAT YOU ALREADY HAVE $

If you can repurpose furniture, decor, and storage items from other parts of your house, you won't have to buy it! Walk through your house (and maybe even the houses of friends and family) and take inventory. See anything you could use? A dresser? A bookshelf? Throw pillows? Baskets or bins for storage? A comfy chair or rocker? Maybe some art or photos for the walls?

Register for Big Nursery Items

Don't forget! Cribs and other of the higher-priced items you want for your nursery are great additions to your baby registry! If it's too much for one person, several friends or family members could go in together.

Secondhand Savvy

Buying gently used items is a great way to save up to 50 percent on items for the nursery. Check your local consignment shop, consignment sales, yard sales, Craigslist, and more for gently used crib sheets, swaddling blankets, mattress protectors, and more.

Sturdy, safe bookshelves, gliders, textiles, and artwork are other great items to find secondhand. Just watch out for lead-based paint. If the furniture is in a color or fabric you're not too fond of, it's amazing what a can of paint or a slipcover can do.

A Note About Going Green in the Nursery

There's been a lot of talk recently about outgassing of volatile organic compounds (VOCs) and semi-volatile compounds from conventional baby products. Suspect nursery items include items with polyurethane foam, waterproof covers, and other items made from some types of vinyl, pressed wood furniture, synthetic carpet, and conventional wall paint.

Only you can determine your comfort level when it comes to possible chemical exposure in the nursery. Learn about this constantly evolving issue and make an informed decision. To learn more, check sites like HealthyChild.org and SafeMama.com. For lists of VOC-free nursery products, try GreenGuard.org and GoodGuide.com.

I've done my best here to present a variety of options to fit different budgets. As you might expect, going all-out green is going to cost you. Fully green alternatives can cost 30 to 1,000 percent more than conventional nursery products.

If there are eco-friendly items you feel you must have but can't afford, try to find them secondhand via Craigslist, eBay, or consignment stores. There are intermediate steps you can take, too, by choosing products that allow you to bypass the most suspect materials without going 100 percent natural.

If you buy standard items, air them out as long as you can (at least until they lose that "new" smell). Buying secondhand, so that much of the outgassing has already occurred, is also an option in some cases. You might also consider using an air purifier to help clean the air. They make great white noise, too.

An Ode to IKEA

The IKEA store near us opened a few months after we set up the nursery. If it had opened a wee bit earlier, you better believe my son's room would have featured some amazing Swedish bargains. We could have picked up a mobile, cute prints for the walls, a crib, a crib mattress, a changing table, and curtains for less than $250. Isn't that amazing? IKEA also carries blankets, bedding, washcloths, high chairs, dishes, bathtubs, toys, and toddler beds. I won't even go into all the other cool decorative stuff in the kids' section at IKEA (and no, they're not paying me to say that).

There are around twenty IKEA stores in the United States, mostly in or near major metropolitan areas. Find your nearest location at www.ikea.com/us. If you're anywhere near a store, you owe it to yourself (and your wallet!) to check it out.

If you're pregnant and plan on heading to IKEA, make sure you wear comfortable shoes and leave yourself time to take a break. On second thought, that's good advice for everybody. IKEA is huge, and there's a lot of standing and walking involved. It's also a good idea to take someone who can do the heavy lifting for you if you end up buying furniture or anything bulky.

Now that we've covered the basics, let's take a look at the individual products most parents want in their child's nursery.

Crib Notes: How to Buy a Great Crib for Less

Crib shopping can be overwhelming for first-time parents on a budget. You want something safe and attractive, but you don't want to spend a mint. Here are some tips to help you save when buying a crib:

Secondhand Cribs?

It's okay to buy a fixed-side crib secondhand as long as you check for recalls and inspect the item thoroughly to make sure it meets current standards and is in great condition. Avoid cribs with peeling or cracked paint, splinters, or loose or missing parts. Avoid drop-side cribs, too. Sales of drop-side cribs were banned in 2010 after too many injuries occurred. Drop-side cribs used to be the most popular choice for parents, and there are a ton of them out there on the secondhand market. Be safe and stick with a fixed-side crib.

Crib Safety Must-Haves

Speaking of safety, the American Academy of Pediatrics (aap.org and healthychildren.org) offers these additional recommendations for choosing a new or secondhand crib:

- When purchasing a crib, look for Juvenile Product Manufacturers Association (JPMA) certification. The JPMA seal indicates that the product has been laboratory tested to ensure that it meets current safety standards.
- The slats should be no more than two and three-eighths inches apart. Widely spaced slats can trap an infant's head.
- All joints and parts should fit tightly.
- The end panels should be solid, without decorative cutouts that can trap an infant's head.
- Corner posts should stop even with the end panels. If they're taller than the end panels, clothing can catch on them. That's a strangulation hazard.

Where to Shop for Your Crib

Try discount stores like Target or Walmart for budget cribs. IKEA is also a popular choice for parents lucky enough to live near one (otherwise, shipping is atrocious or unavailable). Amazon, Overstock, and other online retailers also offer well-priced cribs with free or cheap shipping.

How Much Should You Spend?

Whether you spend a lot or a little on a crib depends on how long you think you'll keep it. If you plan on using the crib with more than one child, or if you'd like to keep it as an heirloom, then by all means buy something with quality construction and materials. If not, it may make sense to go the cheaper route. We picked up the cheapest crib Target had. It was about $100, and it lasted until we were ready to move my son out of it. The most expensive cribs cost upwards of $1,000 or more (crazy!), but it's certainly reasonable to expect to find a quality crib for under $300.

Some parents opt for a convertible crib that can be taken apart and reassembled as a toddler bed, daybed, and/or single bed. These are an option for parents who love their crib's style. They cost more, though. Expect to pay $200 or more.

Like modern decor? Modern cribs can really break the bank, as you'll see when you start to look around, but there are now some less-expensive choices out there. In addition to IKEA's clean-lined cribs, ParkLane and Olivia by Baby Mod (each sell for around $300 at Walmart) are worth a look for parents favoring clean lines.

Buying your crib and mattress together in a bundle can offer fab savings. Walmart recently offered a Graco Lauren crib plus a crib mattress for $145. Other bundles throw in crib bedding, too.

Popular Budget Crib Brands

- Graco
- Baby Mod
- Stork Craft
- DaVinci

Crib Mattresses

Have you ever tried comparison shopping for mattresses? It's darned near impossible since the names change from store to store. Crib mattresses aren't quite as bad, but close. And you do *not* want to make any bad decisions where your darling's sleep is concerned, right? Here's what you need to know to get a good deal, because if you're gonna buy a crib, you're gonna need a crib mattress.

The standard crib mattress is 52" long x 27.5" wide x 5–5.5" high, though each mattress may vary by half an inch or so from this measurement. You'll want to be sure the mattress fits snugly. You should barely be able to fit your finger between the mattress and the side of the crib. Also, be sure to look for the JPMA seal, a sign of quality.

There are two types of mattresses out there, mattresses with foam and mattresses with springs. Both are good, and which one you choose is more a matter of personal preference than quality, as long as the mattress is firm and fits your crib snugly.

When it comes to innerspring mattresses, *Consumer Reports* recommends a mattress with at least 150 coils. Basically, the more coils, the firmer (and heavier!) the mattress. You also want a mattress with border rods that make the edges firm so your baby won't get stuck between the edge of the mattress and the crib—yikes!

When shopping for a foam mattress, look for high density, firmness, and resilience. Foam mattresses, which are made from polyethylene or polyester, may weigh less than coil mattresses. That's a plus when you're changing the sheets.

Parents who want an eco-friendly mattress will look for those made with soybean or natural latex foam, organic cotton batting, and/or wool padding or covers. Naturepedic's No Compromise crib mattresses fit the bill and are highly rated. They cost $250 to $300, which makes them great candidates for your baby registry.

Parents who can't afford the pricier eco-foam mattresses, but who still want to minimize risk, are buying a standard mattress and allowing it to air out for several weeks in a ventilated room and/or wrapping the conventional mattress with a cloth barrier cover (the New Zealand company BabeSafe makes one).

Other parents even opt for a secondhand crib mattress because much of the outgassing has already occurred. Secondhand mattresses have the added benefit of being cheaper, but their use is a bit controversial as they may carry mold spores, allergens, and/or biological contaminants.

Reader Tip

If you can, wait to buy your furniture for the nursery when stores are clearancing out last year's models (usually at the beginning of the year). Target and other stores mark down big-ticket items (cribs, dressers, changing tables, mattresses, and so on) usually during January—buy then! I've found cribs clearanced for 50–75 percent during that clearance time.

—Becky

4 Budget-friendly *and* Eco-friendly Options

These crib mattresses cost less than $200 and allow parents to avoid some of the toxic chemicals I mentioned earlier. In the following mattresses, the petroleum-based foam has been replaced by latex or soybean foam, and/or the mattress cover is organic cotton or nylon rather than vinyl.

- Colgate Eco Classica I Crib Mattress: $150 to $190
- Sealy Soybean Foam-Core Crib Mattress: $100 to $120
- Serta Nightstar Eco Firm Crib and Toddler Mattress: $130 to $140
- Moonlight Slumber Eco-Friendly Little Dreamer One Firmness All Foam Crib Mattress (Yep—that's really its name): around $150

Bedding: Bye-Bye Bumpers and Other Tips

Crib Sheets

Expect to pay $7 to $15 or so for crib sheets. You'll want three (trust me, sometimes you'll go through all three in one night!). Crib sheets should fit snugly on the mattress. Wash crib sheets at least once before using them the first time to remove chemical residues. Organic crib sheets are also a popular option.

Crib sheets are available in a variety of fabrics. Cotton is a classic choice, but some brands are prone to shrinkage, especially if you're washing in hot water. Crib sheets also come in a T-shirt–like jersey material. The great thing about jersey is that it doesn't shrink like regular cotton sheets do. You'll actually be able to put it on your crib mattress after you wash and dry it. Flannel is soft and great for cooler climates. You'll also find sheets in velour and bamboo. Highly rated brands that won't break the bank include Sumersault, Circo (Target), American Baby, and Carter's Easy Fit.

The Ultimate Crib Sheet by Summer Infant and the QuickZip Sheet by Clouds and Stars are relatively new to the market, and although they cost quite a bit more than regular crib sheets, many parents swear by them for easier middle-of-the-night changes. Both come in organic versions as well.

The Ultimate Crib Sheet is a sheet and absorbent waterproof mattress pad in one. It attaches to the bars of the crib with elastic straps and snaps, rather than underneath the mattress. That way, you don't have to lift the mattress to change it. They cost around $25 each.

The QuickZip sheet sets start at around $33. The base fits on the mattress, and the zipper sheet (the part the baby sleeps on) zips off when wet or soiled. You can buy additional zipper sheets for around $19.

Reader Tips

You want as little in the crib with your baby as possible. That means bumpers and blankets are out, so skip the bedding sets. A crib sheet and skirt (if you want one) is all you need. You can always buy breathable bumpers down the road if you decide you want them.

—Leah

I made a crib skirt from one of IKEA's great children's textiles. Very inexpensive to do, and there are *tons* of tutorials online.

—Stephanie

TAKE IT A STEP FURTHER: MAKE YOUR OWN CRIB SHEETS Why not sew your own crib sheets? PrudentBaby.com and Make-Baby-Stuff.com have lots of patterns. Pick up some great fabric and go!

Waterproof Crib Pads

Waterproof crib mattress pads will keep your mattress cleaner. If your mattress cover is waterproof, you can skip them, but you may prefer to have one so that you're not putting a clean crib sheet on top of a wet mattress in the middle of the night. It's a good idea to buy two pads so that you'll have one to put on while the other is in the wash. They can be flat and sit on top of the mattress, or fitted. Whichever you choose, your pad should be thin, so you don't create a puffy sleeping surface. You can pick up a crib mattress pad for as little as $10 or so, with organic options running as much as $80.

Use caution when buying a secondhand crib mattress pad. Standard mattress pads used to contain phthalates (yep, more icky chemicals), which the CPSIA (Consumer Product Safety Improvement Act) banned in 2009. It's also smart to avoid mattress pads made from vinyl (PVC), which can contain harmful chemicals. Polyethylene is a good alternative. Wool is also an eco-friendly option, but keep in mind that you'll have to air- or line-dry it to avoid shrinkage.

Crib Mobiles and Hanging Mobiles

Since babies spend so much time lying on their backs looking up, it makes sense to have a pretty mobile for them to gaze at. What doesn't make sense is how expensive they are: $40 to $50 for a mobile that spins and plays music? Really? And don't forget to add in the cost of all those batteries you'll be putting in it. Why not make one yourself?

Mobiles are easy to make. You're only limited by your imagination. Start with an embroidery hoop and some fishing line. Attach colorful shapes made from felt, wrapping paper, or cardboard and hang it from the ceiling above the crib or changing area. Air movement from heating, air, or fans will make it dance. A quick Internet search for "DIY crib mobile" or "make crib mobile" will turn up lots more ideas. You'll find links to a few at Baby Cheapskate.com (http://bit.ly/DIYmobiles).

If you'd prefer to buy, look for a secondhand mobile or watch for deep discounts on mobiles from brands like Fisher-Price, Manhattan Toy, and Tiny Love. Flensted makes a moderately priced line of modern ceiling mobiles that go on sale fairly often, too. Child of Mine mobiles from Walmart are cute and run about $20. Or browse Etsy.com for adorable handmade crib mobiles and other first toys at great prices.

Reader Tip

I made my own mobile using cardstock, fishing line, and a free geometric pattern I found on the Internet.

—Kristy

Pretty It Up: Decor and Nursery Furniture

Be creative when it comes to artwork for the nursery walls. Making your own can save you big, and don't think you have to be an artist, either. For inspiration, tutorials, and tips, check out the posts at http://bit.ly/budgetnursery. It also pays to keep accessories simple, and maybe even a bit sparse. Nurseries work best when there's plenty of room to move around. Cleanup's a snap, too.

If you're still not convinced that you have the time,

talent, or inclination to make your own art for the nursery, you can pick up some great pieces and prints at great prices from the artists and artisans at Etsy.com.

Murals and Wall Decals

Thinking of adding a hand-painted mural to the nursery? Unless you're an artist yourself, be prepared to pay lots for it—around $50 to $150 per square foot. When deciding on a design, be wary of babyish murals that your child will insist be replaced with rocket ships by the time he's out of preschool.

A thrifty, and less permanent, alternative to a hand-painted mural is to buy some stick-on wall decals. It's as easy as it sounds. They're like giant removable stickers. Keep in mind that decals are best for walls that aren't too textured. I stuck some cool flower decals to the sixty-year-old plaster wall in my bedroom. A couple of weeks later I woke up in the middle of the night hearing the most bizarre sound. Turns out they were slowly peeling themselves off the wall because it wasn't smooth enough for them to adhere properly.

You'll find wall decals in dozens of themes and patterns at discount stores. A set should cost you under $10. You can order custom decals from Etsy.com stores as well. There you'll get to choose your own colors, order decals with your child's name, and so on. Expect them to cost more—up to $50 or so.

5 Ideas for Wall Decor (No Artist Required)

- Trace a simple image or pattern onto paper or stretched canvas (a light box is helpful), fill in the lines with acrylic paint, and hang.
- Staple decorative fabric to a wooden frame and hang.
- Scan, print, and hang covers of or illustrations from vintage children's books.
- Enlarge and hang framed photographs of family members.
- Cut out and paint letters that spell your baby's name.

Curtains and Blinds

"Falling back" for daylight savings time takes on a whole new meaning when you have a little one. Babies tend to wake when it gets light outside, right? So when the time changes and it gets light a whole hour earlier, guess who's going to have to get up a whole hour earlier? You!

Blackout shades in the nursery are a must, in my opinion, if you value sleep. Heck, we layered some cheap stick-on blackout shades (available at home improvement warehouses for less than $10), regular blinds, *and* some dark-colored drapes in an effort to keep the nursery dark. If your windows tend to be drafty, it's also a good idea to choose insulated drapes to help keep the nursery warm in winter.

Check IKEA and discount stores like Walmart and Target for inexpensive drapes. You can always make your own with some fabric and drapery clips, too.

Rug

If you're keeping it simple with the crib bedding, rugs are an easy way to add style to your nursery. Again, I suggest buying one a five-year-old would like so that your nursery will grow with your child. If you must have a theme for younger kids, try to spend less than $50 for a nursery rug. You should be able to do that easily at stores like Target, Walmart, and IKEA.

FLOR carpet tiles, which come in lots of colors and patterns, are also a great choice for hard-surface flooring, with two added benefits. First, if one tile gets stained, simply replace it with a spare and your rug is like new. Second, FLOR tiles are made with low VOCs and no off-gassing chemicals. You can even send them back to FLOR when you're done with them for recycling.

Paint

Choose a low- (or no)-VOC, washable latex paint to avoid breathing in harmful fumes. These paints are more expensive at up to $90 a gallon(!), but they're getting cheaper as more and more options reach the market. Stores like Lowe's and Home Depot carry low- and no-VOC paint for as little as $25 a gallon.

You'll also want to choose a washable paint so that you can wipe down walls without marring the surface. That means most flat paints are out. It's better to go with an eggshell or satin.

> **TAKE IT A STEP FURTHER:** Look for "Oops" paint and save big. Home improvement warehouses discount paints that didn't quite live up to the expectations of the shoppers who ordered them. Take a look at the Oops paint selection; there may be something you love!

Rocker or Glider

Parents with newborns spend a lot of time rocking, jiggling, and bouncing their little bundles, and yet despite conventional wisdom, a rocker or glider is not a necessity in the nursery. In fact, many parents who get one tell me they didn't use theirs nearly as often as they thought they would. Some got more use out of a comfy armchair relocated from another room in the house. Others rocked their babies while sitting on a $15 yoga ball.

Having something comfy to sit on in the nursery is a must. Whatever you choose, you'll want to make sure it's easy to get in and out of with no hands, comfy, quiet, and easy to clean. You'll also want to make sure it's wide enough to let you hold and nurse a baby comfortably.

If you do opt for a rocking chair or glider, choose one that will work well with the rest of your decor so that you can use it elsewhere in the house later. It's also nice to have an ottoman or stool to put your feet up on while you're nursing. Stork Craft makes glider and ottoman sets for around $150. They get good ratings at stores like Amazon .com. Shermag and Dutailier are nice, too, but a bit more expensive. IKEA recently introduced a rocking version of their iconic Poang chair that runs about $169.

Lighting

The single best thing we did in our nursery is to install a dimmer light switch. If you have overhead lighting, a dimmer will allow you to keep the light down during middle-of-the-night changes. If you're not handy, or don't want to pay an electrician to install one, try a table or floor lamp with a few different brightness settings.

Storage

A nursery needs good storage. I'd have to say that the dresser we put in my son's nursery—an eight-drawer model about six feet long and waist-high—was the most useful item we had in there. The dresser was a hand-me-down that we painted bright colors and changed the knobs on. We attached a contoured changing pad to the top, stashed diapers in the drawer under it, and were good to go. My son still uses it.

Dressers are pretty easy to come by, and there's no point in buying one specially made for the nursery. Instead of a kids-only item, choose something that will grow with your child. Jazz up a secondhand dresser with paint and switch the knobs or handles out with something fun. You can even add removable decals for extra pizzazz. Just make sure your secondhand dresser is in good condition, with no flaking paint or splinters, and not too rickety. And be sure it can't tip when pulled on from the front. Attach it to the wall with special clips found in the baby safety aisle or at your local hardware store if you need to.

More B-U-Y than DIY? Shop Craigslist and Freecycle for freebies and cheapies near you. IKEA is also a great source for dressers. I like the ubiquitous Malm line. You can also find inexpensive but stylish dressers under $200 at Overstock.com, Target.com, and elsewhere.

Changing Table, Pad, and Cover

The dedicated changing table is something else you can skip. Attach a contoured changing pad to the top of a dresser, or just change your baby on the floor on a changing mat (they're often included with your diaper bag), blanket, or towel.

Contoured changing pads are foam pads that attach to the top of a piece of furniture with a strap. They also have safety straps to put around baby (but always keep one hand on the little stinker to make sure he doesn't roll off anyway). You can pick up changing pads at just about any store that sells baby products. Summer Infant's contoured changing pad is regularly available at Amazon.com for around $15 on sale. You'll want at least two changing pad covers. Pick them up wherever you find your changing pad. They run about $10 to $15 and come in several fabrics in addition to the traditional terry cloth. There are organic options, too. Handy folks can make their own covers pretty easily. Look for patterns and tutorials online.

Bookcase

Babies have lots of board books, toys, and animal friends, and all this can take up a lot of space. Store them in a bookcase or on shelves borrowed from another room of the house. Or choose one—you guessed it—that will grow with your child. Be sure to attach it to the wall so that it won't tip when baby starts to pull up.

IKEA's Expedit line makes a great bookshelf and toy organizational system. Having cubes rather than shelves makes it easy to keep books and toys where they belong. Add bins for smaller items, and *voilà*!

Baby Monitor

Now that my son's older I can chuckle about how much the baby product industry preys on the fears of inexperienced parents. When I was pregnant I didn't think it was funny at all. I was seriously concerned that if I didn't monitor my baby's every breath and movement, terrible, terrible things would happen. What if he were to accidentally roll over onto his stomach?

Despite my concern (okay, paranoia), I never bought a baby monitor. My son's crib was less than twenty feet from my bed even though he had his own nursery. I have found that I was (and still am, actually) instinctively jolted awake by his every grunt, groan, and whimper. My cutie-pie's never had trouble getting my attention.

If your home is big enough that you'll be out of earshot of your baby's room, or if you find that you're not awakened like I was, you may find a baby monitor pretty useful. You'll just need to decide whether you need to see your baby or whether hearing her is enough.

If you want a basic audio monitor, try a consignment shop, where you can probably pick one up for under $10. Features to look for include an AC adapter to save batteries, multiple channels, and extra receivers.

The most common complaint with audio monitors is poor sound quality due to static or interference from other wireless devices in your home that may use the same frequency. Whatever you buy, make sure you can change frequencies to clear up interference. Sony's BabyCall monitor is a popular choice among parents. It has twenty-seven channels, so you're sure to find one that comes in loud and clear. The BabyCall monitor runs $30 to $40 new.

Another issue to be aware of with monitors is privacy. If your neighbors have a monitor or cordless phone that uses the same frequency, you may hear their baby or their conversations, and vice versa. Buying a digital (DECT) monitor will allow you to avoid this. Philips AVENT monitors with DECT technology guarantee an interference-free connection, though they're quite pricey at around $90.

With video monitors, the most common problem is picture quality. As you'll see from consumer ratings at stores like Amazon, none of them is really stellar. Summer Infant's Best View and Day and Night video monitors are parent favorites. Lorex monitors are also popular. Summer Infant monitors cost about $100 to $150, while Lorex monitors can be found for around $150 on sale.

Planning a Nursery for Multiples

Designing a nursery for multiples when you're on a budget takes considerable creativity and planning, and you'll want to do it a bit sooner than you would a singleton nursery, since some moms end up on bed rest and many multiples are born preterm.

Luckily, there's really no need to buy two of everything. Many parents opt to have multiples share a crib until their babies get too big for it. If you decide to put two or more cribs in the nursery, check out IKEA; the footprint of their cribs is a few inches shorter and narrower than that of many other popular cribs.

The biggest difference between a nursery for one baby and a nursery for multiples is that there's more to be done. Staying organized is key with two babies to change (one at a time, of course), two babies to feed, two babies to comfort. Keeping track of who did what in the middle of the night can be a challenge, so do as one reader did and hang a whiteboard or chalkboard in the nursery to make it easier. Another parent installed a dorm room–style mini fridge in the nursery to save time making bottles. You'll also want to think hard about storage, since you'll have twice as many diapers and wipes to stash.

Additionally, if your nursery is far from where you'll be spending the most time with the babies, set up a satellite changing station near your main living area. It could be as simple as a changing mat, diapers, wipes, and rash cream in a basket. Otherwise, you'll run yourself ragged running back and forth to the nursery to change one baby and then the next. Reader Marcia says that having a Pack 'n Play in the living room with an elevated changing table was a lifesaver.

Reader Tip

If you plan to tandem nurse (nurse two babies at the same time) don't get a traditional glider/rocker with the idea of using it for feedings. I used a glider for almost every single feeding with my first (a singleton) but it was way too small to use with two babies at once. With the twins, I always nursed on our couch or on the bed so I could fit everything (myself, my gigantic nursing pillow, both babies, snacks, water bottle, and notepad to write down feeding times). I would even recommend considering waiting to purchase a chair for the room until you have been home for a little bit and you see what arrangement works best for feed-ings. If you must get something before babies are born, I'd recommend a love seat or larger if space allows.

—Sarah

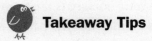 **Takeaway Tips**

Here's a list of the nursery items covered in this chapter, along with some top tips for quick reference. Remember, none of them are "needs," so you should feel free to skip over items that don't fit your lifestyle.

- **Crib:** You should be able to find a quality crib for less than $300. IKEA makes a great line of inexpensive cribs.

- **Crib mattress:** Choose a firm mattress that fits your crib, your budget, and eco-sensibilities.
- **Crib sheets (3):** Consider jersey crib sheets that don't shrink. You can make your own crib sheets for less than you can buy them.
- **Crib pad (2):** A waterproof crib pad can help keep your mattress clean. Beware of secondhand pads with phthalates.
- **Crib mobile:** DIY mobiles give your baby something cute to gaze at for much less. If you want to buy, try secondhand.
- **Dresser:** The dresser is a workhorse in the nursery. Consider a secondhand dresser that can grow with your child.
- **Bookshelf:** A bookshelf can hold lots more than books. Attach yours to the wall to prevent tipping or use wall-mounted shelves to save space.
- **Changing pad:** Contoured changing pads that attach to a dresser can make changing more convenient. You can also change your baby on the floor or anywhere else that's safe with a simple blanket or changing pad underneath.
- **Chair or rocker:** A rocker/glider isn't a necessity, but a comfy place to sit is.
- **Baby monitor:** You may not even need one. If you do, consider other electronic devices that may cause interference.

- **Blinds and/or curtains:** Blackout shades can help your baby (and you) sleep longer.
- **Artwork and other decor items:** Be creative and come up with frugal, one-of-a-kind pieces rather than buying. Wall decals are a great alternative to murals.
- **Lighting:** Install a dimmer in the nursery or use a dimmable lamp.
- **Rug:** Choose a rug that a five-year-old would like in order to prevent having to redecorate too soon. Carpet squares are a great, eco-friendly choice.

Chapter 6

• • •

Feeding Baby for Less:
From Boobies to Bananas

When my son was a newborn my husband and I were a little concerned that we would break him, so we pretty much took every piece of advice that was given. One alarmist parenting book we read suggested that it would be helpful to keep track of what went into or came out of baby just in case . . . something happened. Today, neither my husband nor I can remember why the book said it would be helpful. It sounded like a good idea at the time.

We made a chart, printed out a stack of them, and kept them on a clipboard. We would write on the chart every time he nursed (and for how long, and from which boob), every time he peed, and every time he pooped (noting the consistency and color). If we'd had a scale, I'm pretty sure we would have weighed it just to be sure everything was normal. We were like the castaways on TV's

LOST, pushing the button without knowing why, and desperately hoping the island wouldn't explode.

We were diligent in our milk and poo charting, and probably a little neurotic. I think we missed the part in the book where it said when to stop documenting, so we kept at it until my son was at least five months old. Considering how often babies eat, pee, and poop, you can imagine how tall our stack of charts was by then.

Our neighbors would come over and ask about the clipboard with the two-inch-tall stack of charts, and then look slightly concerned when we told them what we were doing. I think our parents thought we were a little crazy, too. In retrospect, I think we just wanted to feel like we had a handle on those crazy new-parent-with-a-newborn days. As it turns out, everything was A-OK.

Be it from breast, bottle, or spoon, baby's got to eat. Chapter 6 dishes up the savings tips and techniques to help you feed your baby for less (no charts necessary). We'll discuss where to spend and how to save on everything from breast pumps to formula checks to high chairs.

Breastfeeding and Nursing Accessories

Breast milk is best, of course. I have a feeling you already knew that. And it's free, too, right? Yep, but there are some decidedly not-free products that can help make it a whole lot easier and more convenient. Some of the supplies breastfeeding moms may want include the following:

- Breast pump
- Breastfeeding pillow
- Nursing bras
- Breast pads
- Containers to store pumped milk in
- Bottles so someone can help Mom feed the baby

A Mom's Most Valuable Gadget: The Breast Pump

Moms: Do yourself a favor. If you breastfeed, buy a breast pump even if you're a stay-at-home mom who plans to breastfeed exclusively. Why? First, it will allow you to store a few days' worth of milk in the freezer in case you get sick and have to take medication that's not breast-milk friendly. Second, your husband, partner, or caregiver can help feed the baby, and that may translate into a little more sleep (hooray!). I'll stop short of calling a breast pump an absolute essential, since you can express milk by hand if you have to, but an inexpensive pump can make expressing *much* easier and faster.

A pump is even more important for moms who work outside the home. If you do, you just may find that having a good breast pump makes the difference between breastfeeding your baby successfully and having to switch to formula. Here's a rundown of the four types on the market:

Hospital-grade Pumps

If you're pumping exclusively, you'll want to look into renting a hospital-grade pump. These pumps have strong motors that can really cut down the time it takes to pump.

You can rent a pump from a hospital or medical supply store. There's no need to worry about using a pump that another mom has rented before, since rental pumps are specially designed so that the parts that come into contact with milk are part of a closed system and can be replaced or sterilized. Expect to pay around $45 to $65 a month to rent a hospital-grade pump, depending on the model. A deposit may be required as well.

Keep these two things in mind: If you use it for six months, you'll end up paying as much as you would have for a Medela Pump in Style Advanced. Additionally, these pumps can be heavy and awkward to transport, so if you'll be hauling your pump to work, you may want to stick with the double electric pump.

Double Electric Pumps

Double electric pumps allow you to pump both breasts at once—a real time-saver. Most double electric pumps come with a carry bag. If you can, skip the carry bag and use your own instead. You'll save about $100.

Here are three parent favorites:

- The Medela Pump in Style Advanced is about $250.
- The Ameda Purely Yours Breast Pump with carry bag lists for about $225, but can be found on sale pretty easily for about $100 less.
- The Lansinoh Affinity Double Electric Breast Pump is a great budget choice at around $150.

Reader Tip

The double pump cut my pumping time in half. With the kids in the other room I didn't have much time to get it done.

—Amanda

Single Electric Pumps

Expect pumping to take about fifteen minutes per breast. If you'd rather save money than time, go for a single electric pump. They cost less than doubles. Medela's single electric pump lists for about $65, and you should be able to find it on sale for about $50 to $55.

Manual Pumps

If you're a stay-at-home mom who pumps every once and a while rather than every day, you can probably get away with a manual pump. These small mom-powered pumps have no cords or batteries. Three picks:

- The Philips AVENT BPA-Free Manual Breast Pump lists for around $40.
- The Lansinoh Manual Breast Pump lists for around $35.
- The Medela Harmony lists for around $35.

Secondhand Breast Pumps?

Look on Craigslist and you're sure to see used electric breast pumps on sale for a fraction of the cost of a new pump. It seems like a bargain since you can replace the tubing and valves on a secondhand Medela Pump in Style Advanced for under $20. Is it a good idea? Not according to the FDA.

The FDA classifies breast pumps as single-user items. That means they'd prefer you not to buy a used one, even if you *can* replace the tubing. The problem is that particles of breast milk can still come into contact with parts of the pump that you can't replace. As the FDA puts it, "The money you may save by buying a used pump is not worth the health risks to you or your baby" (http://1.usa.gov/usedbreastpumps).

Still, although I can't recommend it here, I've heard from several moms who are happy with their choice to buy and use a secondhand breast pump and replace the tubing, valves, and so on.

3 Ways to Spend Less on a
Double Electric Breast Pump

Double electric pumps are expensive, even on sale. So if picking up a secondhand pump is out, how else can you pay less for one? Here are three ideas:

See if your health insurance provider will cover all or part of the cost of a breast pump or a pump rental (it's classified as "durable medical equipment"). Some will, especially if you have a prescription for one from a pediatrician that shows that it's medically necessary. You may be restricted to certain brands or types, however.

Thanks to a February 2011 ruling, you can also use a pretax FSA (or similar plan) to cover your breast pump and other "supplies that assist lactation" without a note from your doctor (see IRS publication 502). The IRS changes also mean that you can deduct the cost of your pump as a medical expense as long as your medical expenses total more than 7.5 percent of your adjusted gross income (and you itemize). If you're buying the pump in the same tax year as you have your baby, that may well be the case. It was for my family.

WIC has a breast pump program that provides breast pumps for low-income moms. Contact your local WIC office for details.

Where to Buy Your Pump

Breast pumps go on sale just like other baby products. Look for deals on breast pumps at Amazon.com, Target, Walmart, and BreastPumpsDirect.com. Watch for rebates and free gifts to make your savings even sweeter.

Breastfeeding Accessories

Here are a few more items that can make breastfeeding easier:

Breastfeeding pillow. Breastfeeding pillows are designed to help mom cradle the baby while she's feeding (because even a newborn can feel awfully heavy after a while). My Brest Friend and Boppy are two bestselling choices. The Boppy is a firm C-shaped pillow. The My Brest Friend is a little more involved, with a strap that goes around the waist to support the baby even more, elbow rests, and a little storage pocket.

Both pillows are readily available at consignment stores and sales, or look for one new wherever baby products are sold. List price on the Bare Naked (sans cover) Boppy is around $30, but you should be able to find one on sale for less than $25. The covers are around $10. My Brest Friend retails for around $42, and can be found on sale for about $10 less. Covers are around $17. Whichever you choose, you'll need a couple of washable covers. These things are prime targets for spit-up and leaky diapers.

Is a breastfeeding pillow necessary? Nope. They're really only practical to use at home. You can use a regular pillow, too (though I'd put a water-resistant cover on it or make sure it's washable). More experienced breastfeeding moms tend to go without pillows altogether.

> **TAKE IT A STEP FURTHER:** A Boppy is really just a firm C-shaped pillow, and pillows are easy and cheap to make. You'll find a tutorial for making your own C-shaped breastfeeding pillow at Make-Baby-Stuff.com. You'll also find patterns for making covers for it.

Nursing bras. Nursing bras are usually soft-cup bras that either pull down or have flaps to allow baby access to lunch. There are some underwire nursing bras on the market, but many doctors advise against them. You'll want two or three good nursing bras. Shop for them near the end of your pregnancy, when your girls are closest to the size they'll be when baby's here. If you have a sports bra, it may double as a nursing bra.

Look for breathable, washable bras that adjust to fit changing breast size. Bravado, Anita, and Playtex are popular brands. You can also try stores like Target and Walmart. They carry their own lines that cost less. Some parents also like sleep bras because these soft, stretchy bras offer needed support at nighttime. You should have no problem finding one for less than $20. Or make do with a comfortable sports bra or tank.

Hands-free nursing bra. Hands-free nursing bras may look like something from a science-fiction movie, but some multitasking moms swear by them. These bras allow you to hook yourself up to your breast pump flanges and go about your business while the pump does its thing. Most accommodate all major brands of breast pumps, but check the product info to be sure. Readers' favorite is the Simple Wishes Hands Free Breastpump Bra (around $30). This bra gets five stars from over 330 consumers at Amazon, so you know it must be good.

Nursing tops and tanks. Nursing clothing is not necessary, but some parents like nursing tops and tanks because they make breastfeeding in public more convenient. These tops have discreet slits for access to the breast. Some moms complain that nursing tops aren't quite as discreet as they'd like, but instead shout "I'm a nursing mom" to anyone who might be looking. For that reason, many moms tell me they prefer nursing tanks to nursing bras *and* nursing tops. The spaghetti-style straps on some tanks unclip for easy access, while others have cutouts and are designed to be worn under other shirts.

Bravado and Glamourmom make popular nursing

tanks that sell for $45 to $50 (ouch!). Cost-conscious readers really like Target's Gilligan & O'Malley and Liz Lange tanks. They'll run you less than half the cost of premium-brand tanks.

Breast pads (disposable or washable). New moms can be leaky creatures, especially when they first start to nurse. To avoid embarrassing dark circles on your clothes every time you hear a baby cry or are a few minutes late for a feeding, protect bras and shirts from wetness with absorbent breast pads that sit between the breast and bra. Three pairs should be enough. Baby Cheapskate readers like LilyPadz washable pads.

Choose between washable and disposable breast pads. The washable pads are more eco-friendly and can cost less over time if you use them often. You can buy washable cotton, bamboo, or silk pads for around $1 each.

Disposable pads tend to be thinner and come with an adhesive strip to keep them in place. You can also buy disposable pads that are embedded with soothing lanolin. Lansinoh, Philips AVENT, and Medela sell disposable pads for $.10 to $.20 per pad. You should be able to find them wherever you buy baby supplies. Amazon has great deals on them from time to time, too.

Of course, you can DIY as well. The Dr. Sears Web site suggests the simple solution of using a folded cotton handkerchief. You can make your own nursing pads by cutting four-inch circles from cotton cloth, flannel baby blankets (easily available at the thrift store), or cotton diapers. A quick Internet search will turn up several tutorials.

Breast milk storage containers. Breast milk will keep for up to a week in the fridge and up to a month in the freezer. Store pumped milk in glass or BPA-free plastic containers or storage trays with lids, special sterile sealable plastic bags, or baby bottles themselves. The most frugal option, naturally, is to use something you already have in the kitchen.

Lansinoh, Gerber, and Playtex make popular disposable plastic breast milk storage bags. Pick them up wherever you buy formula. They'll run you $.15 to $.40 each depending on the brand.

Look for coupons for these in the goodie bags you receive while pregnant (from stores like Motherhood Maternity and other sources). Lansinoh is also good about sending samples and coupons if you call (800-292-4794) or e-mail them. Wait for a sale and use your coupons then. Amazon.com also has great sales on these that can be combined with their Subscribe & Save discount.

Bottles. Along with a breast pump, I recommend that breastfeeding moms pick up a set of bottles so that someone can help them feed the baby. We'll talk more about bottles in the formula feeding section of this chapter.

Nursing cover. Moms who breastfeed in public often like to have something to cover up with. This could be as simple as a scarf or baby blanket. Just use a clothespin or other kind of clip to attach it to your clothing, or sew on a loop ribbon with a few stitches so that you can wear it around your neck.

There are, of course, lots of commercially made nursing covers out there for up to $40 (for a rectangle of cloth!). Find out how to make your own breastfeeding cover at www.prudentbaby.com.

The Secret Formula for Saving on Baby Formula

If you don't breastfeed exclusively, you'll most likely need infant formula up until your baby is a year old. The cheapest way to buy formula, hands down, is to buy the largest cans or tubs of powdered formula you can find. The price per ounce is much less than ready-to-feed formula or concentrate. The three biggest names in the formula industry are Similac, Enfamil, and Nestlé, the maker of GoodStart formula.

The cost of buying formula can really add up, with a retail price of up to $25 a tub for powdered formula (and even more for specialty, soy, or organic formula). If you figure on going through about one can a week, that's more than $100 a month, and around $1,300 a year. By now you know better than to pay full retail price for formula, right?

It's not hard to pay less. If you live in an area with a few different discount retailers, grocery stores, and drugstores nearby, you can count on finding formula on sale nearly every week. During a good sale, you can get large cans of powdered formula for less than $.80 an ounce ($20 a can). If you have a month's worth of formula stockpiled (it generally keeps for a year), you shouldn't have any trouble waiting until the next good sale to buy.

> **TAKE IT A STEP FURTHER:** To *really* make the most of sales, switch back and forth between brands of formula if you can. My son could switch back and forth between brands with no problem, so we were able to take advantage of any sale that came up. You can mix the formula brands if you're worried about transitioning between brands too abruptly.

Formula Checks and Coupons

The other component of big-time formula savings is formula checks and coupons. Formula checks work much like coupons, but they're technically more like instant rebates. They come in different amounts—$3, $5, even up to $15. Hand the formula checks to the cashier after your order has been rung up and the face value will be deducted from your purchase.

Sign up to receive formula checks at the Web sites of the major formula manufacturers. You'll get coupon checks for about a year after the date you put down as your baby's birthday. Once you have the checks, wait for the sales and use them to stock up on the cheap. Keep an eye on the expiration date, though.

There are also manufacturers' coupons for formula, and you can use them *with* formula checks to save even more. You'll find manufacturers' coupons for formula in newspaper coupon inserts, on manufacturer Web sites, and on printable coupon sites like Coupons.com.

Organic Formula

Whether you buy organic or conventional formula is completely up to you. Proponents of organic food worry about pesticide residues making their way into formula, though science tells us that nonorganic infant formula is safe and free of pesticide residues, antibiotics, and other impurities.

There are many valid reasons for choosing organic products, including "just in case." At the same time, parents who can't afford organic formula shouldn't be worried that they're endangering their children's health. Let your conscience guide you if your wallet permits it. Try a store-brand organic formula to save. Amazon.com also puts Earth's Best organic formula on sale fairly often.

Specialty Formula

If your baby suffers from gas, excessive spit-up, colic, milk allergies, or other conditions, your doctor may advise you to try a specialty formula. Holy moly, specialty formula can be expensive—sometimes up to four times as much as the conventional stuff. Luckily, some insurance companies will reimburse you for the difference in cost between standard and specialty formulas. Here are a few more savings tips:

5 Ways to Save on Specialty Formula

- Ask your pediatrician for samples.
- See if you qualify for WIC.
- Consider buying specialty formula from a reputable dealer on eBay.com.
- Sign up for a program that helps parents afford specialty formula. Enfamil currently has one; it's called Helping Hands for Special Kids.
- Call the formula manufacturers and see if they can help by sending coupons, samples, or formula checks.

Store-brand Formula

Choosing store-brand infant formula over premium brands can save you about 40 percent, or hundreds of dollars a year over premium brands at regular prices. Most major retailers have their own brand of formula, with large cans of powdered formula selling for less than $20. Store-brand formulas are perfectly safe. They're held to the same nutritional and quality standards as premium brands. Store-brand formulas are made by a limited number of manufacturers, so don't be surprised if you find yourself thinking how similar one is to another.

$ QUICK AND EASY SAVINGS $

Check the Top Diaper and Formula Deals of the Week post at BabyCheapskate.com to get the scoop on the best sales, wherever they may be.

Where to Buy Formula

Try to pay less than $.60 an ounce for formula. With sales, formula checks, and manufacturers' coupons, that shouldn't be too hard. Supermarkets and discount stores like Target and Walmart tend to have the best prices on infant formula.

It's possible to find good deals on baby formula online, too. Keep an eye on Amazon.com. Some Baby Cheapskate readers also report finding great deals on formula at warehouse stores like Costco. The can sizes are often larger that what you find at regular stores, so be sure to check the price per ounce to be sure you're getting a great deal.

$ QUICK AND EASY SAVINGS: FORMULA FREEBIES $

Formula samples are readily available. The major formula companies *really* want you to get hooked on their brand, and they're willing to ply you with free goodies to do it. Check formula makers' Web sites for free sample offers. We also received a free sample can of formula in the hospital. You may, too, although some areas have now banned formula samples in hospitals in an effort to encourage breastfeeding.

Your pediatrician is also a great source of samples. *Every* time you go to the pediatrician, ask for formula samples. Don't be shy. Even if you asked for some last time, they won't care! At my ped's checkout desk there were piles of small-size cans of Enfamil and Similac. One of them was packaged in a box with a cool classical music CD and two Fisher-Price blocks. *Free* for the taking! If you're lucky, your baby can switch back and forth between brands, so you can ask for samples of all the brands they have.

Reader Tip

I've had a lot of luck finding new/unopened/unexpired cans of formula through Freecycle! People often get samples in the mail and don't end up using them and pass them on to someone who does!

—Elizabeth

Fill 'Er Up: The Best Baby Bottles

There's a dizzying array of bottles out there, each claiming a specific benefit over all the others. Most parents opt for plastic bottles (BPA-free, of course), though some prefer glass. Many glass bottles currently on the market come with silicone sleeves to prevent breakage. The disadvantage is that they're heavier than plastic bottles. Several major bottle manufacturers make a glass version.

Bottles come in smaller sizes, presumably for newborns who don't drink as much, and larger sizes. I recommend going straight to the larger size. Just don't fill it up as much for younger babies.

Expect to pay $5 to $10 for a bottle. You can probably get away with three of them if you don't mind cleaning them. Buy six if you'd rather go longer between washings.

5 Bottles Worth Buying

- **Adiri Natural Nurser.** This bottle's breastlike shape helps nursing babies avoid nipple confusion. They're about $12 each, but you should be able to find them on sale for under $9.
- **Philips AVENT.** Your basic wide-mouth bottle. Around $5 each.
- **Playtex VentAire Advanced.** A vented, right-angle bottle that claims to keep air out of milk. Under $5 each.
- **Dr. Brown's Natural Flow.** These bottles' special venting system has a great reputation for easing air in the tummy. We used them with my son and were very happy with them. The drawback is that washing them is pretty annoying because they have multiple parts. Around $5 each.
- **Playtex BPA-free Drop-Ins Original.** These classic plastic bottles have disposable drop-in liners that collapse to keep air out of the bottle and your baby's tummy. Around $4 each for the bottles. The liners cost about $.08 each.

Nipples

Bottles really aren't much good without nipples to put on them, so keep their cost in mind as you choose your bottles. Nipples start at around $1.50 each and go up to $5 or more each. A less-expensive bottle generally means a less-expensive nipple. Some brands give you the choice between silicone and latex nipples. Most agree that silicone nipples last longer but are less flexible. Plus, some babies are sensitive or allergic to latex. All nipples will need to be replaced periodically, as they lose shape or the openings enlarge or tear.

Nipples also come in various "flows." The slower-flow nipples have smaller or fewer holes for smaller babies. The faster-flow nipples have larger or more holes for larger babies. Some brands offer adjustable-flow nipples, which allow you to adjust the rate of flow as your baby grows. You'll most likely need to start with the slowest flow for your newborn. If the flow rate is too fast, your baby will cough and choke as the milk comes out faster than she can drink it. Switch to the faster-flow nipple if it seems like your baby is getting frustrated with the slower flow.

Finally, nipples come in three different shapes: traditional bell-shaped nipples; orthodontic nipples, which are made to fit the shape of baby's mouth; and naturally shaped (flat-top) nipples that most closely mimic the shape of the mother's nipple. Babies can be picky. You may have to experiment a bit to see which nipple type your baby prefers.

Baby Food: No Silver Spoon Required

Most babies start eating solid food somewhere between four and six months of age. The American Academy of Pediatrics and other groups recommend that a baby be exclusively breastfed until six months of age. There's no "right" time to start with baby food. When the time comes, you'll decide whether to go with store-bought baby food or make your own.

Infant Cereals

Rice cereal is often the first solid food a baby eats. You can make your own cereal (see below for instructions), or buy it by the box. There are other types of dry cereals as well, including oat and mixed grain. Boxed cereals are often iron-fortified as well. Choose whole grains, rather than white rice cereals, for better nutrition.

Make Your Own Baby Food

If you stop to think about it, baby food is really just regular food mashed up really, really well. Yet it doesn't even occur to so many of us to make our own. It's not even very time-consuming. Baby Cheapskate fans tell me they spend only thirty minutes to two hours total per week making their tots' food. There are several other advantages to making your own food as well:

- You can save money.
- Your baby will get used to eating what you eat.
- You'll know exactly what your baby's eating.
- You'll throw away less packaging and waste.

You don't need special equipment to make your own baby food, either. You *can* spend a lot on fancy food makers or food mills, but there's no need. You can get by just fine with a food processor or blender.

Some parents make baby food right before it's to be eaten, while others take a couple of hours once a week to make a week's worth and then freeze or refrigerate it. Here's the basic how-to:

- Wash and chop food.
- Cook it until soft.
- Mash it or puree it according to your baby's needs (adding a little water if needed).
- Strain it to remove peels, chunks, seeds, and so on, if necessary.
- Pour it into ice cube trays, cover, and freeze for later use. Store frozen cubes in labeled and dated glass or BPA-free containers or bags in the freezer (each cube is about an ounce).
- Thaw, reheat, and eat.

Find out more about making your own baby food, including recipes, at Web sites like WholesomeBabyFood

.com (recipes for baby by age, menus, and more), Weeli cious.com (videos, recipes, and more), and SafeMama.com (a quick guide to finding BPA-free equipment and storage containers).

Those Web sites have tons of (free) recipes, but if you still like browsing through cookbooks, here are some of the newest, most popular baby food books out there. Your local library should carry some of them.

- *Top 100 Baby Purees: 100 Quick and Easy Meals for a Healthy and Happy Baby*, by Annabel Karmel
- *Organic Baby & Toddler Cookbook*, by Lizzie Vann
- *Blender Baby Food: Over 125 Recipes for Healthy Homemade Meals*, by Nicole Young
- *Parenting: Love in Spoonfuls*, by the editors of *Parenting* magazine
- *Cooking for Baby: Wholesome, Homemade, Delicious Foods for 6 to 18 Months*, by Lisa Barnes

Commercial Baby Food

Prefer to buy premade food? Commercial baby food starts at about $.15 an ounce. Babies go through three to six ounces at a sitting, so if you figure on about 18 ounces a day, that's around $40 to $50 a month. If that price leaves a sour taste in your mouth, cut your costs by signing up at the manufacturers' sites to receive coupons and special offers. Then try to use your coupons in conjunction with a sale.

- Gerber: www.gerber.com/login/register.aspx
- Beech-Nut: www.beechnut.com/Special%20Offers
- Nature's Goodness (Del Monte): www.naturesgoodness.com
- Earth's Best: EarthsBest.com
- HappyBaby: www.happybabyfood.com/community/79/126-sign-in
- Sprout: www.sproutbabyfood.com

Grocery stores and discount department stores (like Target and Walmart) tend to have the lowest sale prices on baby food. Amazon.com is also worth a look when it comes to organic baby food.

Organic Baby Food

Organic foods cost about two to three times as much as conventional baby foods. Is it worth it? As with formula, that's up to you. Organic baby foods haven't been proven to be any more nutritious than conventional baby foods, but they do help you limit your child's exposure to traces of fertilizer, antibiotics, hormones, and other harmful substances. Organic farming practices also tend to be easier on the environment.

If you prefer organic baby food, look for less expensive brands like Earth's Best. Most conventional baby food makers also have a line of organic products. Also, check to see if your supermarket makes a store-brand organic.

Parents are really going gaga over the new (and pricey) premium organic baby foods. They come in pouches rather than jars. Favorite brands include HappyBaby, Plum Organics, and Sprout. If you're interested in trying them, look for coupons at manufacturers' Web sites. Amazon has deals on these from time to time as well. Expect to pay about a dollar per pouch.

High Chairs: Do You Really Need One?

Once you start thinking about your baby venturing into the world of solid food, you'll surely start to think about *where* she'll eat it, too. Do you really need a high chair? Nope. What you do need is a safe and sanitary place for your baby to eat.

As with so many other "must-have" baby products, it's surprising how short-lived a high chair is in the household. We had our chair less than a year. Before you know it, your toddler will insist on eating at the table with the family. If you're like me, you'll be glad when that day comes so that you can get rid of the giant lump of plastic that's been taking up way too much room in your kitchen or dining room. Skipping the high chair altogether is definitely worth a thought.

Or how about going straight to a booster seat with a tray? It's an option for kids six months and up. The Fisher-Price Healthy Care Deluxe Booster Seat is a well-loved model (it currently has a five-star rating from over a thousand shoppers on Amazon). The Rainforest Healthy Care Booster has three height adjustments and a dishwasher-safe tray. The back comes off so older kids can use it. Expect to pay $20 to $30 for a booster.

Here's another high chair alternative: The popular Fisher-Price SpaceSaver high chair is like a semi-reclining booster with tray. It straps onto chairs like a booster. Some parents complain, however, that the arms prevent their babies from sitting all the way up to the table. They cost about $50.

There are even chairs that clip or hook on to the edge of your table. Your baby sits in them suspended in midair. Due to recent recalls of these chairs, I can't recommend them.

Reader Tip

I skipped the high chair altogether. As soon as my son was able to sit up by himself, we went to a little booster seat with a tray that attached to the chair. Before the booster seat, we fed him in his bouncy chair reclined a bit. A high chair is too bulky and takes up too much room.

—Lisa

Choosing a Chair

Decided you do want a high chair? Ask yourself these six questions to find the right one for you:

- Is it easy to clean? The fewer crevices there are for food and crumbs to hide in, the happier you'll be. You'll be washing the tray three or more times every day and wiping down the seat almost as often.
- Can you remove the tray easily (preferably with one hand)? You may need to hold something else in your other hand simultaneously (like the baby!).
- Can you strap your child into the seat easily and quickly? At a minimum, high chairs should have a harness that goes around the waist and between the legs. *Always* use the straps. You may also want a chair that has a post between the legs so the child can't slide down.
- Is the seat adjustable to fit your baby's changing body? You don't need a million points of adjustment, but you do need a few. Babies get a lot taller and a lot heavier between, say, six and eighteen months.
- Can you live with how much room it takes up? The safest chairs have the widest bases. In other words,

they're big. Even if you choose a foldable chair, you probably won't put it away very often. Still, you'll be glad to have the option.

- Will you usually feed your child standing up or sitting down? If you think you'll be feeding as you stand up or move around the kitchen, look for a chair that's height-adjustable. You don't want to have to bend over. Conversely, if you'll be sitting down as a family, you don't want the baby in her chair to tower over the table.

A high chair is a great item to pick up used. They're highly cleanable and they easily outlast a single user. We found ours, a Graco, at a kiddie consignment store for half the price it would have been new. Church and neighborhood consignment sales, yard sales, Craigslist, and Freecycle are also good places to look. Be sure to check for safety and recalls. If you prefer a new chair, and have the room to store it for a few months, consider putting a high chair on your registry.

Graco's Contempo high chair is a highly rated choice. It folds for storage. Fisher-Price's high chairs are parent favorites as well. Both cost around $100 on sale. Graco's Mealtime high chair is also a popular choice. It's about $70 on sale. Cosco's Fold Flat high chair is a bargain at under $40 on sale.

You might also think about a convertible high chair. These three-in-one or four-in-one high chairs look like conventional high chairs but convert to a booster when baby's ready to make the transition. The Graco DuoDiner fits the bill. It costs around $130.

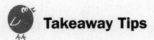 **Takeaway Tips**

This chapter covered the gamut from breastfeeding accessories to high chairs. Here's are some top tips for quick reference:

- You'll probably want a breast pump, regardless of whether you're a stay-at-home mom or work outside the home.
- Breastfeeding pillows aren't necessary, but may be helpful. You can also make your own.
- Buy nursing bras near the end of your pregnancy. Some moms prefer nursing tanks. Two or three should be enough.
- Breast pads can prevent show-through leaking. Choose from washable or disposable.
- Nursing covers can make public feeding more discreet. Or just use a blanket and attach it to your clothing with a clothespin.
- Bottles and nipples come in all shapes. Even if you breastfeed, they can help your husband or partner get involved in feeding. Buy three to six.
- If you'll be using formula, sign up for formula checks

and use them along with coupons while the formula is on sale.

- Making your own baby food is easy and can save you money.
- Sign up to receive coupons on commercial baby food.
- Consider whether you *really* need a high chair.

Chapter 7

• • •

Diapering:
The Bottom Line

Ah, diapering. You'll change around six thousand diapers by the time your baby is two. By the time potty-training time arrives, every parent is bound to have a diaper-related horror story or two, be it the blowout in church, the poop-splattered wall, or the one that's just too shocking to tell at playdates.

Remember my charting story from chapter 6? It shows how diapering can take up *way* too much of your attention. My story's pretty silly, but I know I wasn't alone in the poop obsession. In fact, you can buy specially designed logbooks just for the purpose of charting your little one's poo. There's even an app for that.

Unless your pediatrician recommends it, I vote for skipping the charts, trusting that everything is as it should be, and enjoying your baby. The time is so incredibly brief; why not obsess about your little one's chubby cheeks rather than what comes out of the other end of her?

Okay, focusing on diapering somewhat is unavoidable. It's a dirty job, but somebody has to do it (and do it again and again and again). Deciding whether your baby will wear cloth or disposable diapers (or a combination of both) is but one of the many decisions you'll make while preparing for a baby. The Cloth vs. Disposable diaper debate is a hot one, with each side passionate about its choice. It's a debate I won't be weighing in on here. Instead, in this chapter I'll tell you how to save money on diapering regardless of the route you take.

Diapers Make Great Gifts

Whether you choose cloth or disposable, ask for diapers as baby shower and baby gifts. No, diapers aren't particularly cute or fun, but there's something mighty satisfying about having a closet full of them. Wipes, too.

Cloth Diapering 101

While disposable diaper use is still more popular than cloth diaper use, more and more parents are trying cloth diapers these days. A BabyCenter.com poll of nearly seventy thousand parents (http://bit.ly/diaperpoll) shows that more than a third of them use cloth or a combination of cloth and disposable diapers.

Cloth diapering is the more economical choice. It can save you 50 percent over the first two years of your baby's life, provided you do your own laundering. There *is* a higher up-front cost, however, since you'll need to purchase cloth diapers before the baby arrives if you plan to use them from day one. Cloth diapering start-up costs are around $300, equivalent to around six months of disposables. Expect to spend around $800 over two years to launder them. Another great thing about cloth diapers is that you can often reuse them with subsequent kids or resell them.

Cloth diapering isn't all or nothing, either. You can use cloth when you're at home and disposables when you go out. Or try cloth during the day and disposables at night. To find out more about getting started with cloth diapering, try DiaperPin.com's "How To" page and forums.

Today's cloth diapers are cute and easy to use. There are several different styles and dozens of brands of them, and it's easy to get confused about which type to buy. Luckily, cloth-diapering parents are enthusiastic and helpful folks who will walk you through it. Essentially, you have two choices to make: fitted or one-size, in the all-in-one (AIO) or pocket diaper style.

Choice 1: One-size or Fitted?

One-size diapers are made to fit babies of all sizes. Snaps on the front of the diaper allow you to adjust it to fit babies and toddlers as they grow. One advantage of one-size diapers is that you only have to buy a stash once; you won't ever need to buy a larger size. One-size diapers are also a great choice if you have multiples who don't wear the same size diaper. You can use the same stash and adjust the diaper to fit each baby as needed. There are all-in-one and pocket styles (see below). Examples of one-size diapers include FuzziBunz One-Size and Happy Heinys.

Fitted diapers come in sizes—extra small, small/medium, and large, usually. Like one-size diapers they come in AIO and pocket styles. Because these diapers are sized, some parents feel they offer a better fit and thus are a bit more leakproof. One advantage of fitted diapers is that they remain in better shape for subsequent babies because the sizing means each diaper isn't worn as long. Fitted diapers usually require waterproof covers. Kissaluvs and Thirsties are two examples of fitted cloth diapers.

Choice 2: All-in-One or Pocket?

Pocket diapers are the most widely used kind of cloth diapers. You stuff an absorbent insert into the diaper's pocket before putting it on your baby. These inserts can be made from cotton, hemp, or microfiber. Some pocket diapers have a built-in waterproof cover and some require a separate cover. Two super-popular pocket diapers are bumGenius 4.0 and FuzziBunz.

All-in-One diapers (AIOs) are one-piece diapers that

work a lot like disposable diapers. You don't need a separate cover or soaker insert because they're built right in. Since they're so easy, AIOs are a great choice if you want your child's day-care providers and babysitters to use your cloth diapers. On the other hand, because you can't remove the absorbent material, AIOs can be harder to clean and may take longer to dry. Bumkins and Kissaluvs Marvels are two popular brands.

Hybrid Diapers

Hybrids are like pocket diapers except that they use disposable inserts rather than washable inserts. The inserts are usually flushable, but that doesn't mean you should flush them. Doing so can be tough on your plumbing.

Three major brands of hybrids are gDiapers, Flip, and GroVia. The diapers run anywhere from $15 to $25 each. The disposable inserts cost between a quarter and $.60 each, depending on the brand. Since that's more than the cost of a premium disposable diaper, hybrids can be a pricey way to go. Parents who use hybrid diapers generally do so for ethical reasons rather than to save money. Some hybrid brands also sell a washable insert, allowing parents to fully cloth diaper at home but switch to disposable inserts for use at day care or with babysitters.

Diaper Trial Programs

Still feeling overwhelmed? Relax. There's no need to worry about committing to a particular brand or type of diaper right away. Several retailers offer cloth diaper "trial" packages. These are a great way to get your feet wet and get a feel for the different types and brands of cloth diapers before you make a large investment.

With most trial programs, you pay a refundable deposit plus a trial fee of $10 to $75, depending on the retailer. You get a mix of ten to twelve different types and brands. Try the diapers for three weeks to a month. At the end of the trial period, you keep the diapers you like and ship the other diapers back (at your expense). To find retailers offering cloth diaper trials, just do a quick Internet search for "cloth diaper trial."

How Many and How Much?

Plan on purchasing about eighteen to thirty-six cloth diapers. The precise number you need depends on how convenient it is for you do to laundry. Just remember: Newborns need around a dozen changes per day; toddlers may only need half that number. Your total cost for new diapers will probably be $200 to $300. The nice thing is, you don't have to spend it all at once. Buy a few and use them in conjunction with disposables to see how you like them. Keep adding to your stash until you no longer need to supplement with 'sposies.

How to Save on Cloth Diapers

To save cash on cloth diapers, consider purchasing gently used diapers. You can find them on Craigslist or eBay. Several cloth diapering Web sites also have dedicated forums where you can buy gently used diapers.

Another way to cut costs is to look for sales of "seconds" at the Web sites of diaper manufacturers. And of course, remember to put cloth diapers or gift certificates to cloth diaper retailers on your registry.

Cloth diapers do go on sale, though the discounts retailers offer aren't huge. Check the Facebook pages of your favorite diaper makers or retailers for coupon codes and sale announcements. From time to time, daily deal sites like BabySteals have cloth diapers for up to 50 percent off. Several popular cloth diaper brands also run rebate or free diaper deals from time to time. A recent FuzziBunz campaign, for example, allowed parents to get two free diapers by mail if they purchased six diapers in one transaction.

Reader Tips

While pregnant buy a diaper or two every paycheck.

—Casey

Use cloth diapers! Many are one-sized, meaning you can use them all the way through potty training.

—Emily G.

Buy some used ones in different styles or get a trial package so you can find out what works for you, then you can buy new (on sale, of course) or buy up more used ones in the styles you like. Resell the others that don't work for you.

—Holli

Cloth Diapering Accessories

If you choose to use cloth diapers, you'll probably want some of this stuff, too:

- **Diaper sprayer.** A diaper sprayer is a piece of equipment that connects easily to your toilet for rinsing solids off diapers. You can buy one for $35 to $40 or make your own with one of the tutorials available online. Just search for "make your own diaper sprayer" to find them.
- **Wet bag.** You'll also probably want a small, zippered or drawstring wet bag to store dirty diapers in your diaper bag. Look for them where you buy cloth diapers. You can find really cute inexpensive handmade versions at Etsy.com or make your own (just do a quick Internet search to pull up lots of patterns, or try clothdiaperfoundation.org). Of course, you can

also use a gallon-sized Ziploc. There's no need to throw it away at the end of the day. Just turn it inside out and wash it with some soap and water for reuse.

- **Liners.** Diaper liners go between the diaper and your baby. They help keep poop off the diaper to prevent staining. They can be washable or disposable. You should be able to find liners wherever you buy your cloth diapers.

Disposable Diaper Basics

Brace yourself: If you use disposable diapers, you'll probably spend more than $1,500 on diapers before your child is potty trained and buy enough jumbo packs to fill your house up a couple of times over. The number of diapers babies use per day goes down as they get older. Newborns go through as many as a dozen diaper changes a day, or about 250 to 300 diapers a month, whereas toddlers can usually get by with as few as six changes per day. Don't count on spending less, though. As diapers get larger, you'll pay more for them. Now for the good news: It's easy to save up to 50 percent on disposable diapers if you know how. First, a few diaper-buying facts:

The smallest packs commonly available are jumbo packs. There are also mega packs, big packs (also called big boxes), and value packs. With other products, larger packs usually translate to smaller per unit costs, but with diapers, you can't assume that the larger pack is the better deal. What's more, two jumbos contain roughly the same number of diapers as one big pack, but you can use two coupons when you buy two jumbos, but only one coupon when you buy a big pack.

Figuring the cost per diaper is essential if you want to save money. It's almost impossible to do the per-diaper math in your head, however, given the odd numbers of diapers per pack. Use a calculator (there's probably one on your cell phone) to figure the cost per diaper. Just subtract any coupons you have from the price and divide by the number of diapers per pack.

Diaper Fit and Sizing

A diaper that fits well is a diaper that won't leak as much. Diapers are sized N, 1, 2, 3, 4, 5, and 6, and it's easy to figure out which size to buy. The packs list the weight range on the front. The fit can vary according to brand, though. Here are a few more considerations:

A kid who is difficult to change and moves around a lot when you try to get the diaper on benefits from a stretchy waistband and tabs. You'll also want a diaper that you can unfold with one hand. Plus, if you have a crawler, you'll want a diaper that's not bulky for ease of movement.

Urine leaks are due to either volume or poor fit. Make sure there aren't gaps around the legs or waistband and change the baby frequently. Good double-leg gathers and a high waistband are important for babies with loose or extra-plentiful stools. Need I say more?

And speaking of fit, don't rush to go up a size. The most frugal way to diaper a baby (using disposables) is to keep the baby in the smallest size you can for as long as you can. There are more diapers per pack in smaller-size diapers than larger sizes. A size 3 jumbo pack costs the same as a size 5 jumbo pack, but since there are fewer diapers per pack in the size 5, the cost of each diaper is higher.

Stocking Up: How Many Diapers Do You Need?

Although building a sizeable stash of diapers isn't really necessary (more on why that is in a bit), many parents like to. Parents frequently ask me how many packs of diapers they should buy per size when stocking up. When I was pregnant I was confused about that, too. Then I realized it might be helpful to use a growth chart to predict the weight (and thus diaper size) of a baby at a certain time. I used CDC (Centers for Disease Control) growth charts to find the weight of both girls and boys in the 50th percentile (www.cdc.gov/growthcharts/who_charts.htm) and crunched the numbers. Following is an estimate of how many jumbos of each size you may need if you plan on stocking up or registering for diapers.

Using Growth Charts to Predict Diaper Needs

My son's weight was only in the 5th percentile for much of his first year, so I know that these charts can't predict the weight of *every* baby. Your child's build will have an awful lot to do with how a diaper fits, too. That said, I think the growth charts are a way to form an educated guess about how many packs of each size diaper you'll need. If your kid is in the 25th percentile for weight rather than the 50th, for example, just adjust the data on the list as needed.

- Size N: Six or seven jumbos. Size N diapers generally go up to ten pounds. You'll change diapers *often*, but you won't need this size for long. Buy about a month's worth.
- Size 1: Fifteen-plus jumbos. Size 1 diapers generally go up to fourteen pounds. The baby will reach this weight at around three and a half months.
- Size 2: Twenty-five-plus jumbos. Size 2 diapers generally go up to eighteen pounds. The baby will reach this weight at about seven months.
- Size 3: Seventy-plus jumbos. Up to twenty-eight pounds. The baby will reach this weight at about two years old. You'll be in size 3s for a *long* time.
- Size 4: Forty-plus jumbos. Hopefully this is the last size you'll need. Most kids use this size until they're potty trained.

I've never had a problem switching out a pack of one size for a pack of another size, even without a receipt, so if you find that you've bought too many of a smaller size, just exchange the unopened leftovers.

Shocked at how many diapers you'll be buying? The good news is that because of how the sales work, there's really no need to stockpile beyond about three weeks' worth of diapers. We see great in-store prices at least that often (check the weekly Top Diaper Deal posts at BabyCheap skate.com to find them), and you can save hundreds of dollars by shopping these sales with coupons in hand.

These days you can get some of the best deals on disposable diapers without leaving the house. Buying diapers online can be a real time-saver for harried new parents. Sign up for Amazon Mom at http://amazon.com/mom. As a member, you can save 20 percent off the regular price of disposable diapers when you sign up for Amazon's Subscribe & Save delivery. Shipping is free, too.

Reader Tip

My favorite way to get diapers is through Amazon Mom with Subscribe & Save. . . . We have saved *soooooo* much money getting Pampers through Amazon Mom. We usually get them cheaper than the store brands we tried previously.

—Elisha

3 Rules That Can Save You Hundreds on Premium Diapers

Premium diapers are the Cadillacs of disposables. Competition between the industry giants Pampers and Huggies is fierce, with each company spending billions to convince parents that its product is the superior one. A July 2010 story on ABC's *Nightline*, for example, revealed that at Pampers, more than five hundred scientists, engineers, and others are hard at work on top secret research and development. Each innovation in absorbency, fit, durability, and so on is marketed as revolutionary. It's no wonder that some parents refuse to buy anything but premiums despite the ease and savings offered by store brands.

Premium diapers may be the first diapers to hit the shelves with the latest innovations, but you can bet your bottom dollar that they're the priciest, too. The most popular premium diapers are Pampers Swaddlers (sizes Preemie, Newborn, 1, and 2) and Cruisers (size 3 and up), and Huggies Little Snugglers (sizes Preemie, Newborn, 1, and 2) and Little Movers (size 3 and up). Full price for a premium diaper in size 3 is about $.35. Follow these rules and you can cut that price by up to 50 percent:

Rule 1: Do *Not* Pay Full Price for Premium Diapers

There's absolutely no need to pay full price for premium diapers since they'll be on sale somewhere near you or online each week. When you find a particularly good deal, stock up so that you have a few extra packs, but don't feel like you need to go too crazy. If you're flexible and can switch back and forth between Huggies and Pampers, you only need maybe two weeks' worth of jumbos on hand to avoid having to run out and pay full price.

Premium diapers may be on sale each week, but how do you know when a sale is a *sale*? Common sense tells us that when it comes to diaper buying it really pays to wait for prices to go as low as they will go before you gather up your coupons and head out to buy. Tracking the history of sale prices, we find that currently a good price on a size 3 premium diaper is about $.22 if you shop in-store with a coupon. If you're buying online, you can often find size 3 premiums for around $.19 each, no coupons needed.

Rule 2: Use a Coupon Every Time You Buy Diapers

In more than two years of buying disposable diapers I never had to go without using a coupon for $1 to $1.50 off. You shouldn't either. Coupons are easy to find if you know where to look.

For easy savings, sign up with the diaper manufacturers and they'll send you manufacturers' coupons by mail (start at www.pampers.com/en_US/signup and www.huggies.com). Diaper makers like Seventh Generation and Earth's Best often post coupons on their Web sites, too.

Check the Sunday paper for coupons. You'll find Huggies coupons in the SmartSource newspaper coupon insert roughly once per month. Check Procter & Gamble's monthly brandSAVER coupon insert for Pampers coupons.

Join stores' baby clubs. Target, Babies"R"Us, and some grocery stores have baby clubs. Create a registry and/or join and they'll mail or e-mail you coupons for diapers, wipes, and more. Target sent coupons to our home until my son was almost a year and a half old.

Check for printable coupons online. Sources for printable coupons online include SmartSource.com, Coupons.com, and Shortcuts.com. Money-saving blogs (like Baby Cheapskate.com) often post links to these coupons when they come out. To find them, just search for whatever you're looking for plus "printable coupon" ("Pampers printable coupon," for example). Order the search engine results by date to find the most recent posts.

TAKE IT A STEP FURTHER: If you have trouble finding coupons, try a coupon-trading group like Baby Cheapskate Baby Coupon Traders (http://groups.google.com/group/BCCouponTraders). You can swap coupons you have for coupons you need. Lots of members give away extra coupons, too.

Rule 3: Don't Drive All Over Town for Diapers

Traveling across town in search of a diaper bargain will cut into your savings quickly! Here's why:

The American Automobile Association (AAA) says that the average cost of owning and operating a car in 2011 was 58.5 cents per mile, or nearly $8,776 per year based on 15,000 miles. The cost includes necessary expenses like new tires, insurance, payments, and fuel costs, as well as depreciation. Hard to believe, isn't it?

So does driving two miles extra for diapers essentially add $1.17 to their cost? Not exactly. A few of the costs factored in by the AAA, like car payments and insurance premiums, don't change with a bit of extra mileage. Driving more does mean buying more gas. It also puts extra wear on your tires and on your car's systems. The AAA rates tire wear at .96 cents per mile and fuel costs at 12.34 cents per mile. Routine maintenance is about a nickel a mile. According to the AAA's data, each extra mile you drive costs you nearly 18 extra cents. Drive an SUV or minivan and your operating cost is slightly higher at nearly 23 cents per mile.

The bottom line? According to the AAA's data, paying $9.99 for a jumbo pack a mile from your house is the same as paying $8.99 at a store 5.55 miles away because of the cost of driving. Traveling just six miles out of your way to pick up a pack of diapers (or anything else, for that matter) that's priced a dollar cheaper actually cancels out the savings completely.

Here's an example: According to Google Maps, my nearest CVS is one mile away, but my nearest Target is five miles away. To justify the extra four miles' drive in my small SUV, the price of the item at Target needs to be more than 80 cents cheaper than the price of the identical item at CVS.

I'm not suggesting that you whip out a calculator every time you think about hunting down a sale. You have more important things to do. It is smart, however, to avoid driving across town to try to save a buck.

What About "Greener" Disposable Diapers?

We've seen some interesting new disposable diapers come onto the market over the past few years that claim to be "greener" than earlier choices. Manufacturers have removed the chlorine, made the diapers partially biodegradable, and/or switched in part to organic materials. Some are also latex-free. Many parents whose babies have sensitive skin or allergies choose these diapers because they're less likely to cause skin irritation. Popular brands of eco-friendlier disposable diapers include Seventh Generation, Earth's Best TenderCare, Nature Babycare, and Tushies. Huggies has its own environmentally friendly diaper. Huggies Pure and Natural diapers are made with organic cotton and are hypoallergenic and fragrance-free, but not chlorine-free.

Expect eco-friendlier 'sposies to be pricier than conventional models by about 30 percent. You can find them both online and in-store. Check the manufacturers' Web sites and/or Facebook pages for printable coupons.

Save up to 50 Percent with Store-brand Diapers

If you're serious about saving, then there's absolutely no reason *not* to try store-brand diapers. Finding a store-brand diaper that works for you can mean saving up to 50 percent, or one to two hundred bucks a year over the retail cost of premium brands. Some store brands cost less than $.15 for size 3. Even with the promise of big savings, many parents are afraid to try them. I was.

I don't know what I thought would happen if I tried store-brand diapers. I suppose I envisioned pee running through them like coffee in a filter, soaking baby's clothes, his parents, and the furniture. I won't even describe the horrible poop scenarios I had imagined. But I was brave, readers, and my son's perfect little bum became a product tester.

The fact is, all diapers hold pee and poop. How well

they do so isn't just about the absorbent properties and design of the diaper. A diaper's effectiveness also depends on your baby's size, developmental stage, and elimination specifics. Even if you've tried store brands and been disappointed, try them again. Babies who leak through them at one age may not at another, as body shapes and elimination patterns can change from month to month.

Target and Walmart carry some of the cheapest brands of disposable diapers. Warehouse stores like Sam's Club carry their own brands as well. Store-brand diapers go on sale. It's not uncommon to see buy-one-get-one-free deals on drugstore brands. Watch the circulars or check my Top Diaper and Formula Deals of the Week post at BabyCheapskate.com to find them.

Like most of parenting, deciding between premium disposables and store brands is not an all-or-nothing matter. Even if you only use store brands during the day and stick with premiums at night, you can still save significantly.

What About the Wipes?

About to become a parent? You're gonna need *lots* of wipes . . . ten thousand or so ought to do it for the first two years. Let's talk about how to spend less on them.

Premium Versus Store-brand Wipes

You can save over a hundred dollars a year by buying store-brand wipes at full retail price versus premium-brand wipes at full price. The quality of store-brand wipes is comparable to that of premiums, but the price is roughly half that of premium wipes at nonsale prices. Find out which store-brand wipes cut the mustard by picking up a pack when they're on sale and experimenting. I liked Target brand unscented wipes a lot. They were one of the least-expensive store brands I found.

If you want superthick, clothlike wipes, you'll probably have to stick with premium brands offered by Pampers or Huggies. Luckily, premium-brand wipes go on sale frequently. Watch for the sales and use coupons to try to get your per-wipe price to $.02 or less per wipe. Generally, that means buying your wipes in large packages.

As with disposable premium diapers, one of the best ways to save big currently is through Amazon's Amazon Mom program (http://amazon.com/mom). With Amazon Mom, you save 20 percent off the regular price of disposable wipes when you sign up for Subscribe & Save delivery.

Reader Tip

Once my daughter reached toddlerhood, I began packing wipes in sandwich-sized plastic baggies. I only took about ten or so with me, enough for wiping at diaper changes plus a few extras for hand and face cleanups. This allowed me to buy the wipes in bulk sizes, saving money and effort from not having to spend more money on more convenient to tote around sizes as well as saving me effort in lugging around a weighty diaper bag.

—Jennifer

TAKE IT A STEP FURTHER: CLOTH WIPES Some parents are opting out of buying wipes in favor of making their own. It's really easy and can offer a huge savings. The cleansing solution used on the wipes is usually a mixture of gentle liquid soap, baby-friendly oil, and water. You can find more detailed instructions and lots of recipes by searching for "make your own baby wipes" online.

For disposable homemade wipes, you can use paper towels (thick ones work best; cut the roll in half). Keep the wipes in a plastic container with a lid or reuse a plastic baby wipe tub. You can pour cleansing solution on top or squirt on the solution as you use them.

For washable cloth wipes, use seven- or eight-inch squares of flannel or cut up receiving blankets. Don't sew? Soft baby washcloths work well, too. Also, cloth-diapering retailers usually sell premade cloth wipes.

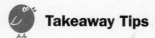 **Takeaway Tips**

- Cloth diapering is easier and more convenient than ever. It can also save you money.
- Sign up for a cloth diaper trial and see how you like different cloth diaper brands.
- Consider buying gently used cloth diapers for extra savings.
- Sign up at diaper company Web sites to receive coupons for disposable diapers, then shop the sales to maximize your savings.
- Try Amazon Mom's Subscribe & Save program for savings on disposable diapers and wipes.
- If you have three weeks' worth of diapers on hand, you shouldn't have any trouble waiting until the next great sale to buy more.
- Don't drive all over town to find diaper deals. With driving costs, you can end up paying more.
- Store-brand diapers and wipes can save you big.

Chapter 8

• • •

Changing Time: Bags, Pails, and Other Diapering Doodads

You just learned a ton about diapers and wipes, but I'll bet you have a few more diapering-related questions. For instance, what should you look for in a diaper bag and what should you put in it? What's the best thing to do with dirty diapers after changing? What's the least gross way to change a baby in public? How can you prevent and treat diaper rash? This chapter will dish the dirt on these topics and more. Let's start things rolling with a little observation.

Moms and moms-to-be: Have you ever noticed how uncomfortable guys are with purses? Next time you're out shopping and head into the dressing room, glance around and see if there are any husbands or boyfriends idling about. Note how they're holding their better half's purse. It cracks me up.

They either hold the purse by the straps with one finger like it's stuffed full of cooties, or they refuse to hold it by the straps at all and clutch the purse awkwardly by its body. The biggest fear, I suppose, is that a buddy or co-worker might spot them and think your bag is something they personally chose because it matched their shoes.

Some guys can be just as funny about diaper bags. When a guy becomes a father he's suddenly expected to do all kinds of things his kid-free friends might see as unmanly, like lug around a diaper bag full of his child's necessities. This eventually led to the invention and subsequent popularity of the "man's diaper bag," which allows guys to skip the "girly" bag in favor of one that sports macho details like camo and skulls. Whatever it takes, right? Of course, if your guy is the type to sport a murse, or "man purse," with pride, you should have no problem convincing him to share the bag you pick out. It's certainly cheaper that way.

Mama Needs a Brand-new Bag (or Does She?): Diaper Bags

Some women love handbags and some don't. Even if you rarely bother with a purse, it's surprisingly easy to get caught up in all the diaper bag madness. Start shopping for a diaper bag and you may notice that some of the priciest are dead ringers for designer handbags, while some of the least expensive can shout "I'm a cheap diaper bag" with their puffy plastic exteriors. That's what makes it all too easy to spend a hundred bucks or more on a diaper bag.

So many of those pricey bags are downright gorgeous! Even now I'm not immune to their charm. Some of those Fleurville and OiOi fabrics make me wish I still needed to carry around diapers and wipes. And Storksak? Don't get me started. But the truth is, there are plenty of diaper bags out there that will do the job for much, much less. And why spend a ton on a bag you'll have little use for in a year or two?

Truly budget-conscious parents will spend $50 or less on a diaper bag. It's really not that hard to find a cute diaper bag for that price. Take a look at bags by Gerber, Trend Lab, Eddie Bauer, Lands' End, Graco, and Jeep. You can find these bags (preferably on sale) at stores like Target, Walmart, and Amazon.

Honestly, you don't *need* a diaper bag at all. Any well-sized tote will do, with the addition of a few items like an insulated bag for bottles and a few gallon-sized Ziplocs for wet items. Or here's another idea: You'll probably get a free diaper bag at the hospital from Similac or Enfamil. Give it a chance; the one I got turned out to be my favorite bag. I kept mine in the car filled with a change of clothing, tissues, Cheerios, and so on.

I had a cute wicker basket in the trunk of my car fully stocked, diapers, wipes, creams, powders, and extra One-sies and a changing pad. I was never far from my car and if I was I threw a diaper and a pack of wipes in my purse. I am a germ freak so I always took my daughter to the car and changed her at my changing station unless we were at a friend's house.

—Brandi

Popular Diaper Bags Under $100

If you really, *really* must have a fancy diaper bag, here are a few parent favorites that still come in at $80 or less:

- **Skip Hop** diaper bags are wildly popular and come in fabulous fabrics. Several models can convert to a stroller bag as well. The Duo Deluxe (find it on sale for less than $30) gets top marks. The extra-roomy Duo Double Deluxe is a favorite for parents of multiples. The Skip Hop Via Backpack ($60 on sale) is another top backpack diaper bag choice. The Skip Hop Dash ($50 on sale) converts from a shoulder bag to a stroller bag. The Via Messenger Bag ($60 on sale) is also a gender-neutral favorite. Skip Hop makes a line of bags specifically for Target called Spark that are all priced under $40.

- **Fleurville** bags, made by JJ Cole, are also a hit, especially Fleurville's Sling Totes and Re-Run Messenger bags. They're pricey at $89, but can usually be found on sale for under $80. The Re-Run's fabric is made from recycled plastic bottles.
- **Diaper Dude** backpacks are gender-neutral and sporty. They cost around $55, and go on sale for as little as $45.
- **JJ Cole Mode** bags are around $55 on sale and feature stylish fabrics and stroller attachments.

Diaper Bag Savings Tips

Watch for the bags to come up on daily deal and flash-sale sites like BabySteals.com, Mamabargains.com, and Zulily .com to save around 50 percent. Just watch out for shipping.

Several brands have periodic warehouse clearance sales or seconds sales online. JJ Cole has one twice a year in spring and fall (jjcolecollections.com). Some manufacturers, like Petunia Pickle Bottom (petuniaoutlet.com), also have online outlets where they sell bags at discounts from time to time.

Most diaper bags can be found on sale or clearance for up to 50 percent off or so. Keep up with the best sales at BabyCheapskate.com and sign up for sales alerts at your favorite retailers.

TAKE IT A STEP FURTHER: If you've got your heart set on a swanky bag that you can't afford, check Craigslist, eBay, and consignment stores for a secondhand bag. You can find them for free sometimes on Freecycle.org.

Diaper Bag Shopping Tips

- Your bag will spend a lot of time on the floors of restaurants and restrooms and on the ground at playgrounds. You'll want it to be waterproof on the outside and wipeable inside and out. Dark colors on the outside hide the dirt better, and light colors on the inside make it easier to find whatever it is that's worked its way to the bottom.
- Backpack diaper bags are great for hands-free travel, but they tend to be smaller than conventional bags. Make sure the bag you choose will hold everything you need to take along.
- Choose a bag that will have a life as a tote, picnic, or pool bag after your baby potty trains.
- Though it may seem counterintuitive, beware of bags with tons of pockets. Unless you have a photographic memory, you'll spend too much time trying to figure out which pocket holds what.

Baby Cheapskate reader Leigh suggests taking everything you plan on carrying with you to the store and test-driving different diaper bag models. Reader Deanna, an experienced mom with three kids, offers this advice: "It must have an adjustable strap so you can wear it close to your body on one shoulder or hanging on your stroller handles. Also, the bottom should be wide enough to stand up on its own when you set it down. A zipper close is great for those times you have to lean over to pick up your baby or step away from the back of your stroller for a minute."

What to Put in Your Diaper Bag

New parents tend to schlep around a *lot* more than they need, while the experienced have narrowed it down to the essentials. Babies themselves are heavy enough, after all. Here's a list that will keep you from having to lug around an enormous diaper bag (and prevent "diaper bag shoulder," too).

Consider keeping a larger assortment of necessary items in the car and only taking the bare essentials with you.

7 Diaper Bag Must-Haves

- Diapers (as many as you think you'll need while you're out, plus a couple extras just in case)

- Small pack of baby wipes
- Place to stash dirty diapers and wipes
- Changing pad
- Change of clothing (extra clothes for you wouldn't be a bad idea, either—spit-up and leaky diapers happen)
- Light blanket (in case baby gets chilly)
- Small bottle of hand sanitizer

And a Few Possible Extras

- Snacks or baby food (depends on your baby's age)
- Diaper cream
- Pacifier
- Burp cloth
- Bottle and formula (possibly) or sippy cup
- Sunblock
- Toy or book to keep baby busy
- Extra breast pads if you're a new and/or nursing mom
- Antibacterial surface wipes

Portable Changing Pad/Mat

You can count on having to change your baby's diaper in public—it's the main reason we carry diaper bags, after all. Many women's and family restrooms have changing stations. Few men's restrooms do, but that's a gripe for another book. If you're like me, you'll look upon the cleanliness and condition of these changing stations with skin-crawling horror and opt for another changing spot. We preferred to change my son in the back of our SUV, but sometimes we had to use those icky restroom spots. That's why I recommend having an adequate portable changing pad or mat with you whenever you're out of the house with your wee one. Antibacterial surface wipes and hand sanitizer are a must, too, in my opinion. To save money on them, buy in large quantities and put a few in a clearly marked Ziploc bag.

Most diaper bags come with a waterproof changing pad, so you won't need to buy one. If yours doesn't, you can spend up to $70 on one at the store, but I don't recommend it (no surprise there, right?). Kushies makes a changing pad for under $10. Summer Infant makes one that's just $5. Munchkin makes a cute mat with pockets for around $15. You can also pick up changing mats at the thrift store for a couple of bucks. You can even use a towel in a pinch. Just make sure whatever you're using is big enough to provide a sanitary changing area for baby. You don't want anybody to have to touch the changing station if they don't have to.

Diaper Pails: The Straight Poop

All diaper pail systems on the market operate under the same principle: Seal in the smell by preventing air movement around the diapers and into the room when you put the dirty diaper in. But here's the thing: Poop stinks. There's no way around it. And if you leave a pile of dirty diapers in your nursery, they're not going to smell like roses, even if you stash them in a fancy diaper pail.

What does cut down on odor? Getting dirty disposable diapers out of the house. Several readers skipped the special diaper pail in favor of a lidded trash can with a foot pedal or just took the diapers straight outside to the trash or straight to the washing machine. Of course, running out to the garage to throw a diaper away may not be so practical during three a.m. diaper duty. For those times, it's helpful to have some kind of diaper receptacle in the nursery.

The three most popular diaper pail systems out there are the Playtex Diaper Genie II Elite (find it on sale for around $40), the Diaper Champ (find it on sale for around $30), and the Diaper Dekor. The Genie and Dekor use special liners and can only be used for disposable diapers. The Champ uses regular trash bags and can be used for either cloth (as a dry pail) or disposables.

Buying special refills for your diaper pail can really add to the cost. Diaper Genie and Dekor refills, for example, will run you $.02 or $.03 per diaper, or more than $180 over the first two years of your baby's life. Regular kitchen trash bags, which you can use with the Diaper Champ, are $.10 to $.20 each, depending on the brand. That comes out to about half a penny per diaper, or about $40 over the first two years of your baby's life—less than a quarter of the price of the special refills. For that reason, I suggest going with the Diaper Champ if you're going to buy a special pail. If you decide to go with a pail that needs refills, watch for sales and coupons.

TAKE IT A STEP FURTHER: Don't turn your nose up at buying a diaper disposal system second-hand from a consignment store. The stores wouldn't have accepted them if they weren't in good condition, and you can cut your costs in half that way. Take it home, wash it out with a little bleach, and you're set.

$ QUICK AND EASY SAVINGS $

Check Amazon for extra Subscribe & Save discounts on Diaper Genie II refills. You can also stock up gratis by putting the refills on your registry.

What to Do with Dirty Cloth Diapers?

If you're using cloth diapers, there are a couple of diaper pail options. Most cloth-diapering parents today use a dry pail, like the Diaper Champ or a lidded trash can. They either shake the solids into the toilet or rinse them before putting them in. Rinsing diapers before tossing them into the wet pail can help prevent stains.

Other parents prefer to store dirty diapers in a hanging wet bag. Hanging bags are fabric bags that hang on a doorknob or hook in the nursery or bathroom. You can find them anywhere you buy cloth diapers. Planet Wise makes a popular version in gorgeous fabrics. Expect to pay less than $25. You can find pretty handmade versions on Etsy.com, too.

Some cloth-diapering parents still prefer the traditional wet pail method. As the name suggests, wet pails contain liquid that the diapers soak in before washing. Parents rinse solids off diapers into the toilet before tossing them into the wet pail to soak. You can add baking soda or vinegar to the soaking liquid to further help prevent odors. A drawback to wet pails is that they're heavy, and lugging them to the laundry room can be a challenge.

Reader Tip

I love the big Planet Wise bags that hang on the doorknob. I have two so when one is in the wash I have a clean one.

—Jasmine

Dealing with Diaper Rash

And speaking of dirty diapers, diaper rash is just about un-avoidable. Sooner or later, most babies end up with a red, sore bottom despite their parents' best efforts, and there are few things worse than seeing your baby scream when you clean her up on the changing mat. What do you do? The best prevention is to keep baby's bum clean and dry. Change her often and allow her to go without a diaper as much as possible.

There are a ton of rash cream and ointment choices on store shelves. Commercial diaper rash creams work by creating a barrier between the skin and the wet diaper. Which one works best? That depends on what kind of rash it is. Diaper rash can be caused by anything from diaper chafing to irritation from wetness to food or chemical sensitivities, so when it comes to commercial diaper rash creams, you'll have to do a little experimenting to see what works best with the diaper rash your little one has. Talk with your baby's pediatrician if you can't get the rash to go away. She's seen a ton of irritated baby bottoms and will offer sage advice. To save on commercial diaper creams and ointments, look for coupons at manufacturers' Web sites and try store brands.

Some Rash Creams Are Bad for Cloth Diapers

Some diaper rash creams can stain cloth diapers or create a coating on them that prevents them from absorbing urine, so to protect your investment, look for one that is free of fish oils and zinc.

Readers' Best Diaper Rash Treatment Tips

I use Calmoseptine (available in the incontinence section of a pharmacy) topped with cornstarch to keep it dry.

—Kristy

When he'll be sitting for a long while in the car, I put a layer of coconut oil on him to stave off any irritation. Works like a charm to keep moisture off the skin, which is what usually causes rashes in the first place.

—Nava

I wash with oatmeal at bath time. Plain old oatmeal. Just put a handful in an old sock or a "pocket" washcloth, soak it in the bathwater, and use it to clean the affected area. You can also use the same solution to wipe the affected area at every diaper change. Works like a charm and it's cloth-friendly.

—Veronica

Our pediatrician had me make up a special cream to combat yeast: 1 part Monistat, 1 part Desitin (or any zinc diaper cream), 1 part cortisone, and 1 part Mylanta. Worked like a charm when other creams didn't.

—Tara

I use good old Vaseline! It creates a great barrier. Also I make sure to let my babies go commando every day for at least ten minutes.

—Avery

Our pediatrician told us to apply Mylanta to cut down on the acidity. We then air-dried (or used a hair dryer on cool setting) and put cornstarch on their bottoms. This worked for us every time. Cheap and easy!

—Kelly

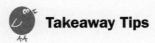 **Takeaway Tips**

- You don't *need* to find a diaper bag. Try to use something you already have.
- Save on trendy bags by shopping secondhand and scouting the sales.
- Make sure you have a portable changing mat for in-public diaper changes. Don't spend much on it, though.
- No diaper pail controls odor 100 percent. Take dirty

diapers outside to the trash or wash them as soon as you can.

- Consider the cost of bag refills when choosing a diaper disposal system.
- Some of the best diaper rash treatments can be made from ingredients you already have.

Chapter 9

• • •

Coming Clean: Baby and the Bathwater

I have pictures of my son's first bath, and boy, do my husband and I look concerned. We're standing at the bathroom counter wearing expressions of intense concentration. I remember that day, and how we gingerly handled our newborn like he was a fragile Ming vase, my husband hovering close behind me as a spotter as I washed and dried the baby. Like most things in parenting, you get a lot more comfortable bathing a newborn after the first couple of times you do it.

Babies are notoriously slippery when wet—and worry about dropping your precious wiggle worm is the last thing a new parent's frazzled nerves need. Jittery parents can rest assured that newborn babies don't need baths every day. Once or twice a week should be fine.

Give your newborn a sponge bath until the umbilical stump falls off and circumcision heals, if applicable. After that, it's bath time (or you can continue sponge baths if you prefer). Some babies take to the water like ducklings, and some don't care for it, so if yours loves the tub, feel free to bathe her as often as you both like . . . and be sure to take lots of embarrassing baby-in-the-bathtub pics during the first year so you can mortify her by showing them to her prom date later.

This chapter comes clean on baby items parents use to bathe their babies: tubs, towels, tub toys, and more. I'll also show you how to pick them up without pouring money down the drain.

Rub-a-Dub-Dub: How to Save on a Tub

You don't *need* a baby bathtub. What you do need is a way to bathe your baby safely. You can bathe your baby in the sink without a tub. Cradle her with one arm and do your washing with the other. If, like me, you're too klutzy to be comfortable with that, or if your baby's too heavy, do as several Baby Cheapskate readers do and bathe your infant by getting into the tub with her.

Reader Kassandra says, "We found that it was easiest to run a full bath and to get in with our little girl. She was more comfortable and it made it easier for her to enjoy the whole process of taking a bath, getting her hair washed, and learning to play in the water without being afraid."

Amber echoes the thought: "First 'real' bath, we tried

the tub we bought at a consignment store . . . she *hated it*! She did not want to lie back (she probably had reflux at the time) and she fussed the entire time. It took both my husband and I to bathe her and we still couldn't . . . do it. She was slipping everywhere. One night, I decided to get in the big tub with her with about two inches of water. We've been doing that ever since. I love that time I get to spend with her, and it relaxes us both before bed. I can easily hold on to her and she loves the closeness. She is much more relaxed and can sit up in my lap. I threw away that baby tub . . . it was nonsense in this household!"

Reader Tips

Readers share a few more tips for bathing baby:

Showering with her was *so much* easier than trying to deal with a squirmy, cold baby in the tub. We got some good skin-to-skin contact for bonding, it stayed nice and warm, all while both of us were getting clean, too!

—Katie

Our routine was to have the tub warm for our little girlie and fill up a dish tub with more warm water and squirtie bottles (from the hospital). . . . I kept one warm washcloth on her belly (to keep her warm even in a small amount of water) and the other I would dip in the warm dish tub to use to wash her. Use the squirtie bottles filled with warm water to wash all the soap off and *voilà*!

Clean little baby. Those squirt bottles are the best for getting the soap off in those little nooks and crannies!

—Jennifer

Choosing a Tub

Prefer to use a tub? Most infant bathtubs are variations of the same model—a sloping back with nonskid foam to keep baby from slipping down. Some have removable slings for really young babies. Extras include temperature sensors, drains, and hanging hooks. You should be able to pick up a good one for $20 or less on sale, new. They're also pretty easy to find on the secondhand market, so check your local Freecycle group, consignment stores and sales, garage sales, and so on, or borrow a tub from a friend.

You can use baby bathtubs in the sink or tub, though unless you're a contortionist by trade, you'll probably find that bathing your baby standing up at the sink is easier at first. It's much easier on the kneecaps and back.

When babies can sit up on their own, you can put them in the sink or tub with a couple of inches of water. Put a towel on the bottom of the sink or tub to reduce the chance of slipping. As always, supervise your baby closely to prevent accidents. Keep your little bathing beauty cozy by making sure the bathroom or kitchen is nice and warm in cooler months.

4 Popular Baby Bathtubs

The First Years Infant to Toddler Tub with Sling is hugely popular, with nearly a thousand reviews averaging 4.5 stars on Amazon. It lists for $23, but you should be able to find it on sale for $18 or less, new. The sling is machine washable.

The **Primo EuroBath Tub** is another top seller. It's big, period, at three feet long, so only consider it if you have a lot of room. Parents love the simplicity of this tub. It's about $25 on sale.

The **Fisher-Price Precious Planet Whale of a Tub** is great for babies up to six months old. It features a removable "ledge" to keep babies from sliding down into the water. It's also pretty cute. List price for this tub is around $26, though you should have no trouble finding it for less.

The Dutch-designed **Tummy Tub** is a new arrival on the market. The Tummy Tub looks like a bucket and allows babies up to six months old to bathe sitting up in warm water, which, say marketers, replicates the womb and leads to blissed-out babes. It runs a pricey $50 or so, though competitor **Prince Lionheart washPOD** is about half the price.

Some moms I've talked to say their babies loved their bucket-style tubs and were very calm during bath time. Another noted positive is that bathwater stays warmer longer in these bucket-type tubs.

On the other hand, other parents say they never used

their Tummy Tub or washPOD much and found that bathing a floppy-headed newborn in it made them too nervous. Another downside parents cited is that when baby's sitting in this position it can be difficult to get to cracks and crevices.

> **Note**
>
> Parents concerned about BPA and phthalates will want to avoid tubs made from PVC (usually the inflatable kind). You'll find a list of acceptable tubs at TheSoftLanding.com (http://bit.ly/safertubs).

Beware the Bath Seat

Bath seats and bath rings, which attach to the tub or sink bottom with suction cups, were responsible for more than five hundred fatal and nonfatal accidents from 1983 to 2010. This led the Consumer Products Safety Commission to issue mandatory safety standards for baby bath seats in May 2010 (www.cpsc.gov/cpscpub/prerel/prhtml10/10237 .html). At that time, the CPSC stated that according to their research, "no baby bath seat currently on the market complies with the new mandatory standard." Check the Juvenile Products Manufacturing Association Web site (www.jpma.org/content/safety/certified-products) to find out which new seats are up to snuff. Or play it safe and avoid them altogether.

Tub Spout Covers

Once your baby gets mobile, you may want to prevent him from bonking his head on the tub spout. Tub spout covers are flexible plastic or rubber sleeves that fit over the spout. A hole on the spout end allows the water to exit. Some spout covers also have a water temperature indicator, but these are generally pretty inaccurate. Some even have bubble bath dispensers.

I say stick with the basic model and avoid pouring your money down the drain. Pick up a simple tub spout cover secondhand at your favorite source or buy one new online or in-store. Skip Hop makes a popular but pricey whale-shaped BPA-free model that sells for $13 and Sassy makes a frog model that can be found on sale for $5 or $6. Be sure to take a look at the spout on your tub before you buy. If your tub spout has a pull-up water diverter, you'll need to choose a spout cover that accounts for it.

Soaps and Shampoos: Tear-free Shopping

Wondering what kind of soap you should use on your baby? You really don't need much of anything for newborns. Tepid or slightly warm water should suffice. For older babies, a gentle soap will do the job for both skin and hair. Look for something advertised as tear-free.

Fragrance-free items are also good for babies with sensitive skin. Readers love California Baby's Super Sensitive products and Burt's Bees Baby Wash. Dr. Bronner's is a less-expensive choice in natural soaps.

Sudsy Savings

To save on baby bath products, try them on sale, and use a coupon at the same time. Coupons from big brands like Aveeno and Johnson & Johnson are widely available. You should be able to find them in the Sunday newspaper coupon inserts, printable coupon sites, and/or companies' Facebook pages. For California Baby and other boutique brands, check Facebook pages and company Web sites for coupons and sale announcements.

And don't toss those free samples you've probably been getting in the mail or in freebie bags. You can use them to see which brands you prefer and save unopened samples for travel.

$ QUICK AND EASY SAVINGS: BABY BATH PRODUCT SIGN-UPS $

Sign up at these Web sites to receive special offers:
- JohnsonsBaby.com/offers
- Aveeno.com/user/register
- Hive.BurtsBees.com/clients/burtsbees/survey. htm

Reader Tip

After the bath, we love slathering the coconut oil on naked baby!! Then he smells like summer, even when it's not (oh, and it makes his skin crazy soft, too). It's great for his little eczema patches, and it makes my hands super soft!

—Amy

Towels That Won't Leave Your Wallet High and Dry

Although there are plenty of them on the market, there's no need to buy special towels or washcloths for babies. Just use something soft that you already have. If you want to make soft baby washcloths, you can cut a flannel receiving blanket into squares.

And while you're at it, skip the baby bathrobes, too. They're perennially on parents' "most useless baby item" lists. After all, how often is your baby going to lounge around in a robe?

TAKE IT A STEP FURTHER: DIY HOODED TOWEL
Hooded bath towels are cute, but pricey at $15 to $20 each for toddler sizes. Make and Takes has an easy, low-sew tutorial for making a hooded bath towel from a regular bath towel and a hand towel. Find it at makeandtakes.com/easy-hooded-bath-towel. Prudent Baby has one for a more luxe version (prudentbaby.com/2011/06/towel-time.html).

Make a Splash: Bath Toys

When your baby becomes interested in toys, he'll go nuts splashing around with a few well-chosen toys in the tub. You'll find that water brings a whole new level of fascination to playtime. Dig through your kitchen drawers for kitchen utensils and empty squeeze bottles that you can repurpose as bath toys. Cups allow tots to experiment with the properties of water by pouring, floating, and measuring. That rubber nasal aspirator you never used also makes a great toy. The same safety standards apply to toys in the bath as they do out of it, of course. Balls and toy boats that float but don't let water inside are also a good choice.

Parents concerned about BPA and phthalates will want to avoid toys made with these products. Boon, Sassy, and i play make some innovative bath toys that fit the bill, and you can find them at stores like Target and Amazon. Consult lists at sites like the Soft Landing and Safe Mama to find nontoxic toys.

Rubber Yuckie!

My son was in the bathtub the other night and gave his rubber duckie a squeeze and it let out a stream of disgusting, chunky, moldy, mildewy gunk. He jumped out of the bathtub completely grossed out.

It's the small hole in the bottom that causes this super-common problem for squeezable bath toys. Water gets in through it and is impossible to get out. It stays in and grows mold (which is also nearly impossible to get out).

Many parents just toss the toys at this point, as did we, though some have reported success cleaning the inside with bleach and water. Your best bet is to avoid toys with these holes in the bottom. Boon makes a rubber duckie without one, if you can't resist this classic bath toy.

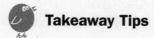 **Takeaway Tips**

- Bathing baby at the sink is a lot more comfortable than bending over a tub.
- Scout for a baby bathtub on the secondhand market to save big.
- Try to buy baby bath washes when they're on sale. Use a coupon, too.
- Look around your house to come up with fun bath toys that don't cost a dime.
- Avoid bath toys that let water inside to prevent icky mold, mildew, and bacteria.

Chapter 10

• • •

Sizing Up Your Baby Clothing Needs

Expectant parents always hear stories of babies outgrowing their clothing in less than a week, but it's hard to believe until you see it happen. Babies. Grow. Like. Weeds. And that's why it doesn't make sense to spend your hard-earned dough on brand-new, tiny designer clothes. Not when it's so easy to get them for free. Of course, as the following story illustrates, some clothing freebies are part of a much larger plan to build brand-loyal babies.

In early 2011, the Walt Disney Company gave out free Disney Cuddly baby bodysuits to moms in more than five hundred hospitals' maternity wards. The bodysuits, which sport licensed Disney characters, were part of a campaign to build Disney brand recognition and loyalty as early as possible. But why wait until baby's born to start? Says a February 2011 *New York Times* article, "[Disney] is working on a loyalty program . . . in which pregnant women might receive free theme park tickets in return for signing up for e-mail alerts" (http://www.nytimes.com/2011/02/07/business/media/07disney.html).

I love freebies as much as the next person, but it's important to see that free bodysuit and those free tickets as the marketing materials they are. If the folks at Disney have their way, your child will sleep on Disney crib sheets, eat Disney baby food from a Disney-themed spoon, and learn to spell M-I-C-K-E-Y M-O-U-S-E as soon as she can speak. They'll cash in big-time when your brand-loyal child begs to go to Walt Disney World earlier than ever.

Of course, most free clothing comes without such strings attached. When we were expecting, my husband and I found ourselves the grateful recipients of boxload after boxload of barely worn baby duds from people we barely know. By the time my son was born, we had put away several boxes of clothes he would wear well after he was walking.

Baby clothes are one thing most parents won't need to worry about buying for baby. Even so, you'll no doubt end up buying something for your bundle of joy, whether it's a coming-home outfit or her first pair of shoes. That's where this chapter will come in handy. You'll learn how to save on baby clothing through smart strategies like buying ahead, buying secondhand, and timing your purchases to coincide with mega-sales. You'll also discover which clothing brands offer the best value for the money and how to recoup your cost by reselling your baby's clothing.

Hooray for Free Baby Clothes!

Filling your baby's closet for free should be pretty easy. Don't be surprised if experienced parents come out of the woodwork and practically beg you to take their outgrown baby clothes off their hands. On the off chance that you find yourself donor-challenged, enlist your mom, friends, and coworkers to go out and solicit baby clothes. Post a sign in your office lounge, OB's office, church, wherever someone will let you. People will *want* to give you their old baby clothes, trust me! And generally they'd much rather give that box to a pregnant lady—even one they don't know—than to an impersonal thrift store.

The odds are pretty good that you'll start your life as a parent with more free baby clothes than you know what to do with. Freecycle.org and your local Craigslist freebie board will help you fill in any gaps. Once you've stocked up, be sure to pass on the love. Pass on what you don't want to another expectant mom, or donate extra clothing to your local women's shelter, clothes closet, or DFACS.

What Does a Newborn Need, Anyway?

Oh, okay, who am I kidding? You may get a lot for free, but who can possibly resist browsing aisles of miniature dresses, sweaters, and overalls? When the shopping urge hits, head to the thrift store. Because young babies grow at lightning speed, thrift store racks tend to be chock-full of brand-new and barely worn clothing. Don't be surprised if you see outfits with the tags still on. Why spend $10 or more on a dress when you can pay $2 for the same thing at Goodwill? Just be sure to check for recalls.

Should You Register for Clothing?

Because you can get so many clothes for free and at deep discounts on the secondhand market, you don't need to put clothing on your baby registry—a few sleep sacks or swaddling blankets, perhaps, but not clothing. Save your registry space for the big-ticket items. You'll no doubt still get lots of wee clothes at your baby shower, though. Your guests won't be able to help themselves.

Layette for Less

"Layette" is just a funny word for the items your newborn will wear. Look at the "must-have" layette list on baby stores' registry guides and you'll see dozens of items. Many of them are far from essential. Is a homecoming quilt a necessity? I don't think so.

Instead of going nuts with a list put out by folks who want nothing more than for you to buy, buy, buy, think about how you'll live with your baby during the first two to three weeks after birth. Where will you go? What will you do? Chances are, you'll be staying at home a good deal. Any newborn clothing you have should meet those needs. Anything else will just be outgrown.

The specific clothing items you really need for your newborn depends on how hot or cold it is outside when she's born as well as how often and under what conditions you'll be taking her into the elements. And don't over-prepare, either. Skip the wee swimsuit, for instance, unless you know you'll be going to the pool or beach. You can always run out and get something if you need it.

You can also skip the teeny tiny shoes. Babies can't walk, so they don't need them. A pair of socks will do just fine in cooler weather. In warm weather, opt for bare feet. They make for better piggy kissing!

Tiny Hangers

It never occurred to me that I wouldn't be able to hang my son's tiny clothes on regular hangers. Be sure to keep any hangers that come with clothing you receive. Thrift stores and consignment sales are great places to score those little hangers on the cheap.

Newborns in general don't need that much, and summer babies can get away with the least. My son, a July baby born into the heat of an Atlanta summer, got away with wearing short-sleeve bodysuits or tees and a diaper most of the time. At night, he slept in a cotton sleep sack or swaddled in a cotton blanket wearing only a diaper. When we went out, we dressed him in a cute bodysuit, shorts, or overalls.

Here's what your baby will need for daytime. Add to this list of essentials as necessary.

Summer Babies

- Cotton tees or bodysuits
- A few outfits for heading out on the town
- Cotton socks (tube-sock styles stay on best)
- Drool/spit-up bibs

Winter Babies

- Long-sleeved bodysuits
- Pull-on pants
- Fleece hat
- A couple of outfits for going out

Reader Tip

A reader shares how to keep baby cozy in cold weather:

Fleece jammies and any long-sleeve/long-pants outfits are what we used in Central Wisconsin. I found jackets and snowsuits to be a waste, since there were very few times they were outside and not in their infant car seats (and it's not safe . . . to put a baby or child in a seat with a winter jacket on). We covered them with a light blanket, put a cute hat on their head, and then covered the seat with a car seat cover. Outfits with footies are always a good option, because babies tend to lose their socks quite often, and you don't want that to happen when it's forty below zero!

—Annamarie

Again, what you'll want to have on hand for a winter newborn depends on how often you expect to be out in the weather. NYC parents sans car have different needs from their counterparts in suburban Illinois. And keep in mind that your baby will be inside the majority of the time.

Unless you primarily get around on foot, you can probably skip the snowsuit and heavy buntings. Layers are key, for any degree of cool weather. Fleece sleepers, sleep sacks, and hats are favorites among parents in colder climes. A cozy "shower cap"–style car seat cover comes in handy, too. And fleece buntings from JJ Cole are fab for cold-weather stroller outings.

Winter Coats and Car Seat Safety

Heavy coats and car seat covers that come between your child and the car seat or harness are a no-no. The puffy fabric reduces the effectiveness of the seat should you be involved in a crash. Your little one should wear indoor clothing in the car seat. Buckle her in and cover her with a blanket.

How Many of Each?

How many you need of each little item depends on how often you care to do laundry. Expect newborns to go through a handful of outfits each day. Figure on wanting four to eight of each everyday item (bodysuits, tees, stretchies, and so on). Whether it's spit-up or diaper blowouts, babies are messy. In fact, it's a scientific fact that the amount of messiness is directly proportional to the specialness of the occasion. Portrait session? Fancy dinner? Be ready for a serious diaper disaster. And do yourself a favor. Choose clothing for newborns that's easy to change and *always* have a spare outfit with you. It doesn't hurt to have a change of clothes for Mom or Dad, either.

As these reader stories illustrate, when it comes to babies and outfits, Murphy's Law is in full effect:

On my baby's first Sunday back to church, it was Easter Sunday. We got her in her pretty dress and were getting ready to walk out the door. She spit up everywhere and it was all over the dress because Daddy said, "She didn't need a bib." Well, got that cleaned up to look somewhat decent . . . on the way to the car she poops and it explodes everywhere. Easter dress no more. She went to church in a Onesie.

—Amber

I was taking the kids to the doctor and dressed them matching for the first time. I took them outside and sat them down to take a picture. My newborn spit up just as I was snapping the picture. We got home afterward and before we were able to leave to our next destination he threw up enough to coat his entire outfit. The next day I tried again with another outfit they both have and my daughter vomited before she was fully dressed. I replaced her tee, he vomited a bit later, and I gave up!

—Leah

What About PJ's?

Bag-type gowns, wearable blankets, and sleep sacks make for easy diaper access during middle-of-the-night diaper changes. Popular brands include Halo, aden + anais, Summer Infant, and BreathableBaby. Most brands carry cotton and microfleece options. Wearable blankets cost around $20 to $40 each, depending on the brand, but you can easily find them on sale for up to 50 percent off. Find them secondhand for even less.

A Few Other Items

- **Drool bibs.** Some babies are serious droolers, and some aren't. My son certainly was. Our little leaky faucet had to wear a drool bib at all times, and went through them at the rate of one per hour, even more when he was teething. Drool bibs are small cotton bibs that usually attach with Velcro. They're also essential for saving those cute outfits from milk spit-up. You'll probably receive some as gifts. If not, it's good to have a few on hand.
- **Baby leg warmers and arm warmers.** When it's cool outside, baby leg warmers can make diaper changes easier since they allow you to change your baby without taking off pants. They can also help you extend the life of summer clothing by adding arms and legs. You'll find baby leg warmers from BabyLegs and i play for $12 (regular price). BabyLegs has fabulous clearance sales at their Web site, where you can find cute styles for 50 to 75 percent off.
- **Bodysuits.** Baby bodysuits and tees come in an array of styles. Many babies dislike having clothing pulled over their heads. Side-snap or kimono-style bodysuits

and tees let you avoid upset. I asked Baby Cheap-skate readers which bodysuits they preferred, and among the fifty-one responses I got, Carter's was the clear favorite, especially for tall and/or slim babies. They say they're easy to find and hold up well. Pick up Carter's bodysuits in multiples at stores like Target, Kohl's, and Amazon. Or online at Carters.com. They cost a budget-friendly $2 to $4 each.

- **Garment extenders.** If you find your baby's bodysuits getting too short in the stride, try a set of garment extenders. They have two rows of snaps that snap onto the crotch snaps of bodysuits and other baby clothes and extend the length of the bodysuit a bit. Add a Size and i play brand extenders cost a dollar or two each. You can find them at baby clothing retailers and online at stores like Amazon.com.

Reader Tips

Buying layette items for multiples is a bit more involved than simply buying two of everything. Check out these tips on clothing needs for twins, triplets, and beyond, straight from parents of multiples themselves:

Don't buy a ton of matching outfits in the same size . . . my triplets are all in different sizes and we've had a lot of stuff go to waste that we bought before they were born.

—Judy

Some stores offer a multiples discount—ask if your favorite local stores do. Often, even if they don't officially, they will offer a discount if you purchase two of the same item or they will extend a courtesy coupon. Ask, ask, ask!

—Kris

For newborns specifically, don't spend a lot on outfits other than a going-home outfit and maybe one or two special ones. Chances are you won't get out much in the beginning and they'll live in Onesies and sleepers for the first months. Plus, you won't really have time to dress three little babies in a four-piece outfit and then have to undress them for every diaper change when out and about.

—Judy

Think ahead before you are too far along in your pregnancy and shop at consignment sales. The best ones are held by Mothers or Parents of Multiples clubs because there are usually doubles of most things. I would recommend purchasing a good supply of preemie-sized clothing since there is a good chance the babies will be born early. Each store carries very few outfits in this size, so we wound up driving around to all of them as soon as I got out of the hospital. I would also recommend many, many Onesies. You can't imagine how many you go through in a day.

—Lori

A Note About Flame Retardants

Flame retardants are chemicals known as PBDEs that are sprayed on clothing or bonded onto fabric to prevent burn-related injuries and deaths. There is growing concern about their safety, as some studies have shown some flame retardants to cause cancer or disrupt endocrine systems. Yikes!

In the United States, pajamas for kids nine months and older that are made from synthetic fabrics (like fleece) are required to have flame retardants. You can avoid chemical flame retardants by sticking with cottons and other natural fibers. Check the tags for the words "not flame resistant" or "should fit snugly" to be sure. If you're buying online, the product page should also provide this information.

Saving on Organic Baby Clothing

Organic cotton clothing is made from cotton that has been grown without pesticides or herbicides. If dressing your baby in organic clothing is important to you, you should have an easy time finding it. However, it is generally quite a bit more expensive than conventional baby wear, with a long-sleeved organic bodysuit costing $20 to $30, versus around $6 for one made with conventional materials.

There are a few more reasonably priced brands. Gerber, Carter's, and other big-time bodysuit makers offer an organic line. Walmart carries a well-priced line of organic layette items, and Target's current Organics by Tadpoles line is a good value, too. You can also check stores like Amazon for organic baby clothing on sale.

Sizing It Up and Stocking Up

For the uninitiated, baby clothing comes in sizes Newborn (N), 3m, 6m, 9m, 12m, 18m, and 24m. Rather than accumulating newborn-sized clothing that will be outgrown in a flash, it makes sense to stock up on 3m and 6m clothing. Keep in mind that some brands run larger or smaller than others. Check the tag or online product page for weight and height guidelines.

Complicating matters when it comes to stocking up on clothing is that babies come in all shapes and sizes, too. Some babies are long and slim, while others are little chubsters. *And* their body shape can change within only a few months. My son was tall and slim for the first year, and Gymboree brand clothes ran really large for him. Old Navy clothing fit him much better. Experiment and you're sure to find a brand that works well for your baby.

How to Save Big by Buying Ahead

Stocking up on baby clothing is a great way to save money. Scour your favorite secondhand sources for cute clothes at 50 percent or more off retail. If you simply must buy new clothing, shop several months to a year ahead. You'll find the best deals on summer clothing during clearance sales after July 4, so stock up on shorts and tees for the following year then. Score the best deals on next year's winter wear just as the first flowers are starting to bloom.

The drawback to buying ahead is that you're never quite sure what size your baby or toddler will be when it's time to wear the items. Don't let that stop you, though. If you buy something and it doesn't fit, resell it or swap it for something that does at a swap meet or online swapping site like SwapBabyGoods.com.

Keep Your Stockpile Organized

The trick with stocking up is to stay organized so that you don't overbuy or forget what you have. Box up your bargains, label the outside of the box with what's in it, and pop the box in the top of the closet, garage, or attic. As the seasons approach, take that season's box down and go through it to remind yourself of what you have before you buy anything else.

Reader Tips

I organize the clothing . . . in bins labeled with the size, gender, and season. The next year, I go through my bins to figure out if I need to buy anything for that season. Doing this has really cut down on my clothing expenses.

—Kristen

We went to places like Ross, Marshalls, and T.J.Maxx and raided their clearance sections. Their prices are already a percentage from regular retail price, and you can get *huge* deals in the clearance section. We have a large closet, so we were able to hang the clothes up according to size.

—Kara

Favorite Brands and Stores

You can't beat the convenience of buying online. It's easy to find coupon codes and you don't have to schlep all your baby stuff around town. On the other hand, you can browse the clearance racks when shopping in-store, and sometimes it's just nice to get out of the house for a while. Whether you shop online or in-store is completely up to you.

So where do savvy parents go to find great deals on baby clothing? In a poll on BabyCheapskate.com, nearly fifteen hundred parents answered the question "Which of the following brands of baby/toddler clothing do you feel provides the most value for the money?" Carter's and sister store OshKosh B'Gosh were the clear parent favorites, followed by (in this order) The Children's Place, Target brand (Cherokee, Circo, and so on), Old Navy, Gymboree, and Gap.

What About Washing?

Do you need pricey baby laundry soap? Nope. Most babies can get away with one of the "Free and Clear" laundry soaps you can find just about anywhere.

This Little Piggy: Baby's First Shoes

Before you know it, your baby will take her or his first steps (sniff, sniff)! When that happens, it's time for that first pair of shoes. Shoes for brand-new bipeds are different from shoes for the rest of us. You'll want to choose shoes that are flexible (both the uppers and soles), breathable, and have a bit of wiggle room. The soles should be thin enough so that your toddler can feel the ground beneath her feet. They should be easy to get on and hard to kick off.

Many parents prefer to buy shoes in-store so they can have their tots try them on. You can score some fabulous deals online, though. Competition is tough among online shoe stores and that helps keep prices down. Free shipping and free returns are the norm, and you shouldn't expect any less. Many stores also offer low-price guarantees up to 115 percent. This also helps to keep prices uniformly low. Look for deals on shoes online at 6pm.com, Shoes.com, Amazon.com, Piperlime.com, and other retailers. Always check for a coupon code before you buy.

When buying shoes online, be sure to check the store's return policy. Try to choose a store that won't make you pay for return shipping. With some stores, like Target, you can buy online and return most items to a store near you to avoid a trip to the post office.

Finding Baby Shoes That Fit Your Budget

Kids' feet grow really quickly, so don't be tempted to buy pricey brands, even if you have a thing for cute shoes and a closet full of them yourself. You'll just have to shop for them again in a month or two. Try to pay less than $25 for your child's first pair of shoes. Although the shoes I list below cost more than $25, you should be able to find them for under that pretty easily if you know where to look. Most kid shoe brands go on sale fairly often with savings of up to 50 percent.

A Few Favorite First Shoe Brands

- **Robeez** (and Robeez knockoffs) are soft leather shoes with soft leather soles. They fit kids with wide feet, too. Name brands like Robeez and Bobux cost up to $30, but you should never have to pay that much. Sales throughout the year at stores like Amazon allow you to pick up a pair of Robeez Soft Soles for well under $20. Store-brand Robeez-style shoes, available at stores like Target, will run you about $15.

- **Pediped** is another popular first-shoe choice, though a bit pricier. Also fine for kids with wide feet, Pediped features a leather sole with memory foam. The sole's a bit thicker than that of Robeez-style shoes and thus offers a little more protection on rough and/or cold ground.

- **Stride Rite** refers to their line of flexible toddler footwear as "Step 2." More structured than either Robeez or Pediped (and thus less like going barefoot), Stride Rite Step 2 shoes come in actual sizes rather than age ranges. The shoes can cost a whopping $45 new, but with a little detective work you can expect to find Stride Rites on sale for less than $20.

- **See Kai Run** shoes are fashionable and flexible, with a wide toe box for early walkers. They list for about $30 but can be found on sale for as low as $15.

- Other appropriate—and way cute—options are **Pedoodles** and **Squeakers** (both around $30). Both are made from soft leather. Squeakers have removable, well, squeakers that help parents know where their little explorer is.

Resell and Recoup the Cost

One way to slash your net baby clothing cost is to resell outgrown baby clothes at consignment stores. If you got a lot of great stuff for free, you may even be able to make a little money on that, too. Most consignment stores begin accepting fall clothing at the beginning of August and the beginning of March (and that's when you can start picking up some fantastic deals on summer consignment clearance, by the way). I did some research at our local kiddie consignment shops, and here are some guidelines for preparing clothing and so on for consignment:

A good guideline that I've come across at a few stores is to take a good look at your outgrown clothing and ask yourself, "What would I give as a gift?" Consignment stores are emphatic that they are "not thrift stores." Items brought in should be clean and ready to go on the racks (pressed, if necessary). They should be flawless, with no stains, fading, missing buttons, or other flaws. They should also still be fashionable.

So where do you take your stuff? Family-oriented

phone directories, free local parenting magazines, and word of mouth are great places to discover what consignment stores are near you. Visit a few to get a feel for their angle. Some consider themselves upscale and will turn up their noses at your Old Navy stuff in favor of fancy French labels. Others prefer major brands like Carter's but shun discount store labels, and still others accept everything.

Once you've narrowed down your list of possible stores, check their consignment policies. Most stores advertise that they sell for a third to a half off retail prices. You can expect to receive 40 to 60 percent of what the item sells for. Usually, your stuff stays at the store for about two months before it either goes on clearance or you're asked to come get it. Some stores only pay you when you rack up a certain amount on your account, say $50. Sometimes you get better deals if you're willing to accept store credit over cash. Some stores, like Kid-to-Kid, actually buy your stuff outright, so that you leave the store with cash in hand.

You'll need to call the store to find out if you need to make an appointment to bring in clothing. Some only accept items on certain days of the week. While you're on the phone, ask whether they prefer clothing on hangers or folded neatly. Find out what items they currently need and don't need. Many stores, for example, don't have much room for equipment, and some don't take pajamas and other sleepwear.

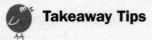 **Takeaway Tips**

- You don't need to register for baby clothes.
- Newborn-sized clothing will be outgrown quickly, so you don't need much of it.
- Think about how you'll live with your baby during the first few weeks. Then buy clothes for that lifestyle.
- Babies don't need shoes until they start walking. Choose flexible, breathable shoes for your baby's first pair, and don't pay too much.
- Stock up on larger sizes at big discounts. Keep your stash organized with labeled bins or boxes.
- Recoup some of your clothing costs by selling or consigning outgrown clothing.

PART THREE

Gear and Other Goodies

Chapter 11

• • •

Cruising: Car Seats 101

In part 2 we covered everything you might want or need to have on hand in order to meet your baby's day-to-day needs at home. Now let's venture out of the house a bit and talk about a few things you might want when you head out to show off that gorgeous baby. For the next two chapters we're on the go. This chapter's about car seats, and the next is about strollers and baby carriers.

First, a little car seat history: Like many of you, I grew up at a time when it was perfectly acceptable to protect your toddler in a car simply by throwing out "the mother arm" when coming to an abrupt stop. I bet you know what I mean. You rode in the front seat (strapped in by a lap belt at most), and when Mom felt you were in danger of flying through the windshield or crashing your forehead into the dashboard, she quickly and authoritatively extended her straight arm across your body. It made you feel very safe.

At other times in my early childhood I rode sideways

in the tiny back compartment (over the engine) of a 1970s-era VW bug, sat in a grown-up's lap, and even rode in the open bed of a pickup truck. And of course there were long driving trips to Florida that passed quickly as I slept stretched out in the back of our huge family sedan.

It's not that child safety seats weren't available back then—it's just that everyday families weren't convinced they were necessary. Who needed to spend money on a car seat when you had the mother arm, after all? It wasn't until the mid-1980s that the National Highway Traffic Safety Administration mandated their use and the majority of babies and young children were strapped into car seats. It's a wonder any of us survived to adulthood.

Times have sure changed. Today car seat safety is a hot topic, and of course it should be. There are dozens and dozens of infant car seats on the market, and you'll need to have one of them safely installed in your car before they even let you drive your baby home from the hospital.

Researching and choosing a car seat can be overwhelming for rookie parents. All the seats for sale today meet minimum government safety standards. Which one's really best, and how much do you have to spend to get it?

Car Seats: A Crash Course

Infant or Convertible?

You don't *have* to get an infant seat. As long as your baby's shoulders reach or are above the bottom harness slots, you can get by with a rear-facing (ride with the seat facing the back of the car) convertible seat. Check the minimum weight and height requirements before you buy. Many parents prefer an infant, or "bucket," seat because they can transport the baby, sleeping or awake, without removing him from the seat—and as all new parents know, when the baby's asleep, you'll do just about anything to keep him that way. Plus, infant seats allow your baby to ride in a reclining position and can fit a tiny baby's body more snugly. Whichever you choose (I'll discuss both types), your car seat will rear-face. It's the safest way for your precious cargo to travel.

You can use an infant car seat for anywhere from a few months to a year or so. Most babies outgrow their infant seats when they reach twenty-two to thirty-five pounds and up to thirty-two inches long or so. Growth charts put the average baby hitting those marks at about a year old. In my experience, once a baby is able to sit up, she'll want to sit up, which is pretty hard to do strapped into a bucket seat. Learning to sit up usually occurs long before a baby outgrows an infant seat.

Before you invest in an infant or convertible car seat, be sure you're familiar with these terms and topics:

LATCH

What's all the fuss about LATCH, anyway? Well, in the olden days, you used your car's seat belts to strap in a car seat. Since 2002, most new cars come with the LATCH (Lower Anchors and Tethers for CHildren) system, which consists of two lower car seat anchors and a top tether. You can still use the seat-belt method to install a new car seat, so if you have an older car, don't worry.

Car Seats Expire!

Did you know that car seats have expiration dates? They certainly do! The materials the seat and straps are made from crack, warp, fray, and just plain wear out over time. Plus, technology and opinions about safety evolve over time.

Most seats are good for five to eight years from the date they're made (not the date you bought it). Look for a seat's expiration date on the bottom of the seat. It may be stamped into the plastic or on a sticker.

Free Installation Inspections

A huge percentage of the car seats on the road today are installed incorrectly. Have your seat installation inspected by someone who knows what he or she is doing. Contact your local Child Passenger Safety Inspection Station.

Is It Okay to Use a Secondhand Car Seat?

Using a secondhand seat is okay *only* under certain circumstances. You don't want to use a car seat that came from someone you don't know. The seat could have been in a crash—even a minor one—and suffered damage that compromises its safety. You also want to make sure the seat isn't past its expiration date or recalled.

If you know the entire history of the seat without a doubt, if you have access to the manual so that you can make sure you're installing it correctly and have all the parts and straps, *and* if you can verify the seat is not expired or close to expiration, it's probably okay to use a used seat. That's a lot of *ifs*.

> ### Which Is Better, Middle of the Backseat or Side?
>
> Most experts agree that the center of the rear seat is the safest place for a car seat. Opt for the center unless your seat can't be secured safely there.

My Fave Car Seat Safety Resources

These five Web sites are invaluable resources for parents researching car seats:

- **NHTSA's Child Safety site:** www.nhtsa.gov/Safety/CPS. Use this site to find a free car seat inspection station near you. This page also links to NHTSA's Ease-of-Use Car Seat ratings.
- **American Academy of Pediatrics' Healthy Children site** keeps parents up-to-date on the newest safety guidelines. Find car seat safety information at http://bit.ly/aapcarseats.
- The car seat that's best for you is the seat that fits your child *and* your car the best. The experts at **Car-Seat.org** can help you find a seat with the right fit for your vehicle. **Car-Safety.org** is another great site.
- **The Car Seat Lady** (thecarseatlady.wordpress.com), a pediatrician in real life, delivers sage advice on car seats on her blog and on her Facebook page.

Choosing and Saving on Infant Car Seats

When choosing an infant car seat, there are a few important considerations:

- 5-point harness
- Front harness adjuster
- EPS foam
- Extra bases available for your other car(s)
- Compatible with your stroller

Other considerations include whether the car seat cover is machine washable and/or dryable and whether the straps will need to be rethreaded after washing or as your baby grows. You'll also want to think about the weight of your seat if you have notions of carrying it around a lot. The lightest infant seat can weigh a full five pounds less than the heaviest seat. That five pounds counts!

Reader Tips

Readers share how they found the perfect seat:

We wanted a reputable brand that would have 5-point harnessing as long as possible. I read reviews online (both *Consumer Reports*-type and parent reviews), I talked to other parents to see what they liked/hated, and then I watched for a sale. The day after Thanksgiving everything fell into place and we bought our seat. That was five years ago and I still use the same technique now that I'm buying for our second child.

—Heather

We found a local car-seat tech through carseat.org and peppered her with questions specific to our setup (three across on one bench seat). She had tremendous knowledge on different seats and was so helpful in locating narrow infant seats for our tight fit and a larger convertible seat to keep our oldest rear-facing as long as possible.

—Stephanie

Ask all your friends, pay attention to people in the mall, and scope them out at baby stores. Play with them, touch the fabric, feel the handle, try out the recline, pull the harness in and out, and try it in your car. If you do all that, it's likely that you won't make a mistake and get something you hate. The biggest money waster is buying a car seat and hating it so much that you have to buy a different replacement car seat.

—Robin

Save or Splurge?

What's the difference between a seat that costs $75 and one that costs $275? First, rest assured that all seats on the market today pass safety tests, so don't feel bad if you can't afford a top-of-the-line seat. Expect more expensive seats to have more bells and whistles, like more padding, easier LATCH connectors, or a better canopy.

The more expensive seats tend to have higher weight limits, too, though that may not be as important as you think. Many parents tell me their tykes were out of their infant seats long before the weight limit of even the cheaper seats was reached. Unless you've got a chunky monkey, springing for the higher-weight-limit seat may not be the smartest financial move.

When choosing a car seat, whether infant or convertible, think about how your baby will use it. Do you travel by car a lot? How long is your average errand-running trip? Families that don't spend much time on the road don't necessarily need a seat with the best padding, but if Grandma lives three hours away and you visit her twice a month, you may want to spring for it.

When it comes to convertible seats, you'll most likely want to buy one for each car your family owns. They don't necessarily need to be the same seat, though. We have two cars, but my son rode in just one of them probably 85 percent of the time. We opted for a cheaper seat for the car we didn't use as often.

$ QUICK AND EASY TIPS
FOR SAVING BIG $

To save on your infant seat watch your favorite retailers for sales or coupons. Prices on the same car seat can vary widely according to fabric or pattern, so try to look at all the patterns before you get your heart set on one. The Chicco KeyFit 30 in the Adventure pattern, for example, is easy to find on sale for around $155, whereas the same seat in Midori is hard to find for less than $175.

You can often cut costs if you find a travel system comprising the infant seat you want plus the stroller you want. The Chicco Cortina travel system in Fuego, for example, retails for about $330. It's made up of the KeyFit 30 infant seat and the highly regarded Cortina stroller. Bought separately, you'll pay $360 for the same car seat and stroller.

Where to Shop

Amazon, Walmart, Target, and AlbeeBaby.com are my go-to sites for finding great deals on strollers. Readers also like Buy Buy Baby. You never know where a great sale will spring up, though, so keep an eye on your favorite money-saving blogs to get the scoop on car seat deals. Be sure to take shipping into consideration as you're comparing prices.

5 Favorite Infant Seats

Below, I've listed readers' favorite infant car seats, along with the list price. Nobody should pay list price, though, right? So I've also listed what I consider the "buy" price— the price point you can expect to find the seat at when on sale. Remember, the more flexible you are about color and pattern, the more likely you are to find these seats at the buy price.

- **Chicco KeyFit 30:** Lists for $180. Try to buy it at $140 or less.
- **Baby Trend Flex-Loc:** Lists for $120 to $130. Try to buy at $90 or less.
- **Combi Shuttle 33:** Lists for $180. Try to buy at $165 or less.
- **Britax Chaperone:** Lists for $230. Try to buy at $175 or less.
- **Safety 1st onBoard 35 Air:** Lists for $160. Try to buy at $130 or less.

Convertible Car Seats: Safety and Savings

When choosing an infant seat get one that will allow your child to rear-face as long as possible. Current guidelines recommend rear-facing at least until age two. And don't worry about what kids are going to do with their legs. They manage just fine.

Reader Tips

Baby Cheapskate parents rave about the Chicco Key-Fit 30:

I swear by my Chicco KeyFit 30. Easy to install, straps are easily tightened or loosened and it washes up well!

—Marina

Chicco KeyFit 30 was wonderful! Lasted until I felt comfortable with a convertible, stood up well to lots of use, stayed clean, baby loved it, and still looks brand-new after a year of use!

—Ali

Best Convertible Car Seats Under $150

In the lists below I've given you the retail price along with what my research and experience tell me is a good price for the seat.

- **Cosco Scenera 40RF:** Try to pay $75 or less.
- **First Years True Fit,** in Casino: Lists for $200. Both the Premier and Recline versions of the seat get fab Ease-of-Use ratings. Try to pay $140 or less.

- **Evenflo Tribute 5**, in Kristy: Lists for $70. Try to pay $56 or less.
- **Evenflo Triumph 65 LX:** Lists for $150. Try to pay $130 or less.

Favorite Convertible Car Seats Over $150

- **Diono Radian XTSL:** Lists for $300. Try to buy at $225 or less.
- **Safety 1st Complete Air 65 LX:** Lists for $199.99. Try to buy at $175 or less.
- **Recaro ProRIDE**, in Midnight: Lists for $280. Try to buy at $260 or less.
- **Britax Marathon 70,** in Onyx: Lists for $280. Try to find it on sale for $210 or less.
- **Britax Boulevard 70,** in Onyx: Lists for $320. Try to find it on sale for $140 or less.

Short on Backseat Space?

Need to fit several seats across in the backseat? Diono (formerly Sunshine Kids) Radian is one of the narrowest seats out there.

Takeaway Tips

- It's generally safest *not* to buy a secondhand car seat.
- Consider your driving needs when choosing a seat. There's no need to splurge on a super-plush seat if your baby won't be sitting in it for long periods.
- There are lots of great Web sites out there that can help you choose a seat that fits your lifestyle, your baby, and your car well.
- Free safety inspections can ensure that you have your car seat installed properly.
- Plan on having your child rear-face until at least age two.

Chapter 12

• • •

Hoofing It: Strollers and Baby Carriers

If you find yourself with a fussy baby on your hands, or if you're feeling stir-crazy, take a walk! A little fresh air and exercise can solve a world of ills. You'll most likely want a stroller, carrier, or both for travel on foot. Even a seven-pound baby can get awfully heavy awfully quickly. In this chapter, I'll show you how to wrangle the baby and all her accoutrements around town without losing your mind . . . or your cute diaper bag.

The number of strollers and carriers on the market has skyrocketed over the past decade, and the price parents are willing to pay for them has, too. We can blame that on the Bugaboo. In *Parenting, Inc.*, Pamela Paul reports that the average cost of a stroller in 2003 was $170. In fact, it was pretty hard to spend over $300 if you wanted to (pages 180 & 182. Times Books. Kindle Edition). A Buga-

boo showed up on *Sex and the City* in 2002 (http://www
.salon.com/life/feature/2004/08/09/stroller).

Soon after, a handful of attractive celebrities were
spotted with Bugaboos and sales took off. The Bug frenzy
spawned a handful of similarly exclusive strollers, the
Stokke Xplory for one, and the stroller price ceiling was
suddenly raised to $1,000 or so. The result? Any parent
from Manhattan to Modesto interested in looking stylish
had better be prepared to pay double what they would
have before the Bug's arrival.

Strollers

Ah, strollers. These days, they're as much playground sta-
tus symbol as they are practical pieces of baby gear. Few
people interested in appearances are willing to have the
cheapest stroller on the playground. That's why so many
first-time parents fall victim to stroller envy, despite their
best budgetary intentions. And once they succumb, it's
awfully hard for them to fess up to overspending.

Many a mom has told me that the particular $500
stroller she bought was absolutely worth it. Nothing costing less would have fit in the car, managed uneven side-
walks, held up to her child's Goldfish habit. I guess there's
a possibility that's true for a few select folks. But to me it
sounds a lot like justification.

As we'll see in this chapter, there are lots of perfectly

good—and attractive—strollers out there at more reasonable prices. Before I tell you about them, take a look at the types of strollers that are out there:

Types of Strollers

- **Umbrella.** Very lightweight and compact. Great for travel.
- **Lightweight.** More substantial than an umbrella stroller, but still streamlined and easy to pick up.
- **Standard.** More bells and whistles than the umbrella or lightweight stroller. More comfy, too.
- **Full-sized.** The big daddy of strollers. Usually pretty hefty and sturdy, with cup holders galore.
- **Jogger.** Made for parents on the run. Literally. Common features include lockable swivel wheel or fixed wheel, hand break, and air-filled tires for all-terrain use.
- **Ride-on.** Allows for one child to sit and one child, usually an older sibling, to ride standing on the back.
- **Infant car seat carrier.** A metal frame that your infant car seat snaps on to. Only useful while your baby can use the infant seat. Because its use is so limited, I don't recommend buying one new.

As with car seats, there's no one stroller that will serve each family's needs perfectly. Think about your lifestyle. How often, where, and under what conditions will you be pushing the stroller? We used ours primarily for neighborhood walks on fairly level paved roads, so our stroller needs were different from those of a parent hoofing it around a big city without a car. If you jog, you'll want a stroller that will allow you to do that safely and comfortably. And if you'll be pushing more than one kid, well, you'll obviously need to buy a stroller with more than one seat.

That brings us to the next question: How many strollers do you need, anyway? The answer is zero, since you can certainly travel without one. They do up the convenience ante considerably, though, so I'm guessing you'll want to procure at least one. Again, it really depends on your lifestyle. A jogger with a wide wheelbase will have a hard time making it through the aisles of your favorite local toy store. Try to find a stroller that's suitable for as many situations as possible.

Some people go a little stroller crazy. Baby Cheapskate reader Amy is one of them:

I admit, we have three strollers. Well, we borrowed a Snap N Go when he was an infant, got a Bumbleride Flyer (which we *love*!!), then got a Maclaren Quest when he was around ten months. I recently purchased a BOB Revolution at a rummage sale to use for running (because I recently started running). I love all three and they all have specific uses. Wouldn't know which one to give up!

I've even talked with readers who have five, six, even seven strollers. Of course, most say they really only use one or two of them frequently. It's typical for families to start with one or two strollers, and then buy another as their child grows. Plan carefully to minimize your stroller expenses—and stroller storage needs.

Strolling with a Newborn

Newborns' floppy heads and inability to sit up mean you can't just plop them in any old stroller. You can buy a car seat stroller frame, a stroller that will accept your infant car seat, or you can buy a stroller with a full recline. A fourth alternative is to skip the stroller for the first few months and opt to use a baby carrier instead.

Parents' Top Stroller Shopping Requirements

I asked Baby Cheapskate readers what stroller features were on their must-have list when stroller shopping. Here are their top requirements:

- Recline
- Basket size
- One-hand fold
- Lightweight
- Compact fold

- Maneuverability
- Easy to clean
- Weight limit
- Visual appeal
- Compatible with car seat

TAKE IT A STEP FURTHER: BUY SECONDHAND

Buying a secondhand stroller is a great way to save 50 percent, 75 percent, or even more. Check garage sales, Craigslist, consignment sales, and consignment stores for gently used models at a fraction of the cost of new strollers. A recent check of my local Craigslist stroller offerings turned up a one-year-old Chicco Cortina for $70 (lists for $180) and a City Mini Double stroller for $200 (lists for $430), along with dozens more. As always, check for recalls, and be sure the stroller is in good working order. You can usually find stroller manuals at the manufacturer's Web site if it's missing. If you can't find it there, call the manufacturer and ask for one.

Saving on a New Stroller

By now you know how it works: Wait for a great sale to buy your stroller and use a coupon code if you can. A few brands, BOB and some Baby Jogger models, go on sale infrequently, however—usually only a few times a year.

Find out about sales on these strollers from your favorite frugal blogs. Set up price watches and subscribe to sale alerts at your favorite retailers to find them. Watch for sale announcements at retailers' Facebook pages, too. Another way to save on a rarely discounted stroller is to buy the previous year's model on closeout. And remember, if it's in good condition, you can recoup the cost of your stroller by reselling it after your child's outgrown it.

Baby Cheapskate Readers' Top 5 Strollers

Baby Cheapskate readers are passionate about their strollers, and here's the short list of the strollers they love:

- BOB Revolution
- Chicco Cortina
- Baby Jogger City Mini
- Maclaren Volo
- Maclaren Triumph

Playground Recon

Take your stroller research a step further with a little recon of your own. Visit a local playground or other attraction popular with babies and toddlers. What strollers do you see? Ask parents there how they feel about their strollers.

Top Strollers by Budget

The strollers on the lists below made the cut because readers adore them. They also get great reviews from both consumers and experts (for a list of sites that offer consumer and expert reviews, see chapter 2). Research the strollers on this list at manufacturers' Web sites with your top four stroller must-have requirements and your lifestyle in mind. Visit stores and test-drive floor models.

In the lists below, you'll note two prices (just as you saw in the car seat chapter). The first is the list price, and the second is the price I want you to pay for the stroller, the buy price. To come up with these prices, I studied past sale prices of each stroller model to see how low the price goes during a typical sale. With a little patience and smart shopping, you should be able to match or beat the buy price.

Best Strollers Under $100

Whether you're searching for a stroller to keep at Grandma's house or you're just truly budget-conscious, you'll be happy to know that you can pick up each of the strollers on this list for less than $100.

- **Chicco Ct0.6 Capri:** Umbrella stroller. Only eleven pounds and comes in lots of yummy colors. Thirty-seven pounds maximum weight. For babies six months and up. List price: $70. Buy price: $60.

- **The First Years Ignite:** Umbrella stroller. Five reclining positions and fifty pounds maximum weight. Around $55 on sale. List price: $60. Buy price: $52.
- **Maclaren Volo:** Umbrella stroller. Good for babies six months and up. High weight limit (fifty-five pounds) makes it great for bigger kids, too. List price: $130. Buy price: $99.
- **Kolcraft Contours Lite:** Lightweight stroller. Big storage basket. Forty pounds maximum weight. Reclines so that it can be used with newborns. List price: $100. Buy price: $55.
- **Graco LiteRider:** Lightweight stroller. Accepts Graco infant car seats. Forty pounds maximum weight. Around $45 on sale. List price: $170. Buy price: $45.
- **Jeep Cherokee Sport:** Lightweight stroller. Does not accept infant car seats. Forty pounds maximum weight. List price: $80. Buy price: $50.
- **Graco Alano,** in Ally: Lightweight stroller. Maximum weight forty pounds. Accepts Graco infant car seats. List price: $100. Buy price: $80.
- **Baby Trend Snap N Go:** Car seat stroller. Accepts most infant car seats. List price: $75. Buy price: $55.
- **Baby Trend Expedition:** Sport stroller. Locking swivel wheel. Fifty pounds maximum weight. List price: $110. Buy price: $90.

Best Strollers Over $100

- **UPPABaby G-Lite:** Umbrella stroller. For babies six months and up. Only 8.3 pounds. Forty pounds maximum weight. List price: $120. Buy price: $110.
- **Graco MetroLite:** Lightweight stroller. Accepts Graco infant car seats. Forty to fifty pounds maximum weight, depending on model. Fully reclining seat. List price: $130 to $170. Buy price: $110 to $140.
- **Baby Jogger City Mini:** Lightweight stroller. Easy fold. Reclines to near flat position. Fifty pounds maximum weight. List price: $240. Buy price: $195.
- **Chicco Cortina:** Standard stroller. Fits popular Chicco KeyFit infant car seats. Fully reclining seat. Fifty pounds maximum weight. List price: $180. Buy price: $152.
- **Graco Quattro Tour Deluxe:** Full-sized stroller with all the bells and whistles. Plush ride, but somewhat heavy. Fifty pounds maximum weight. Fully reclining seat. List price: $160. Buy price: $135.
- **BOB Revolution SE:** Sport stroller. Locking swivel front wheel. Seventy-pound weight limit. Car seat adapter available. List price: $450. Buy price: $383.
- **Maclaren Techno XT:** Lightweight stroller. Offers full recline. Fifty-five pounds maximum weight. List price: $320. Buy price: $291.
- **Maclaren Triumph:** Lightweight stroller for babies

six months and up. Fifty-five pounds maximum weight. List price: $170 to $250. Buy price: $150.

- **Kolcraft Contours Options 3-Wheel II:** Reversible seat. Infant car seat attachment fits most brands. Seat can recline fully. Fifty pounds maximum weight. List price: $180. Buy price: $115.

Strollers for Two

Tandem strollers, where the tots sit front to back, and side-by-side strollers are nearly equal in popularity, with slightly more parents preferring side-by-sides. Tandem strollers can prevent bickering between siblings and can be easier to store, while side-by-sides allow both kids a front-seat view and give parents easy access to both kids. Both can be awkward to push.

Best Double and Tandem Strollers

- **Graco Twin IPO:** Side-by-side. Umbrella. Fifty pounds per child maximum weight. List price: $190. Buy price: $170.
- **Maclaren Twin Triumph:** Umbrella. Side-by-side. Fifty-five pounds per child maximum weight. List price: $265. Buy price: $210.
- **Maclaren Twin Techno:** Umbrella. Side-by-side. Fifty-five pounds per child maximum weight. List price: $380. Buy price: $356.

- **Graco Duoglider LX:** Tandem. Lightweight. Forty pounds per child maximum weight. Can fit infant car seats. List price: $170. Buy price: $150.
- **Baby Jogger City Mini Double:** Side-by-side. Lightweight. Fifty pounds per child maximum weight. List price: $430. Buy price: $344.
- **Kolcraft Contours Options Tandem:** Standard. Forty pounds per child maximum weight. Can fit infant car seats. List price: $260. Buy price: $170.
- **Chicco Cortina Together Double:** Tandem. Standard. Forty pounds per child maximum weight. Can fit infant car seats. List price: $300. Buy price: $273.
- **Graco Quattro Tour Duo**, in Clairmont: Tandem. Full-sized. Fifty pounds per child maximum weight. Can fit infant car seats. List price: $250. Buy price: $190.
- **BOB Revolution SE Duallie:** Sport. Side-by-side. Fifty pounds per child maximum weight. Infant car seat adapter available. List price: $660 (MAP pricing). Buy price: $527.

Reader Tips

Do Baby Cheapskate readers prefer tandem or side-by-side double strollers?

I like the side by side more so both babies can see everything. I just had to find one that would fit through doors.

—Maureen

Front to back! I can't imagine trying to maneuver a side by side in a store or through a crowd!

—Kristi

I think each has its own good and bad qualities. I loved the [tandem] when my second son was born because my older son was not able to mess with him. Now I want a side by side since we are walking more and starting to jog with them.

—Jackie

Baby Carriers

Babies spend nine-plus months carried around by their moms 24/7. It's no wonder so many babies are soothed by being worn in baby carriers. A baby that cries less is a good thing (can I get an *amen*?). Plus, there are places where strollers just can't go without a lot of hassle, like public buses, for example. And last but not least, when baby's in the carrier, parents get the convenience of using their hands for something other than carrying the baby.

Babywearing, as it's known, is as old as time itself. There are an awful lot of newfangled carriers today to make it easier and more comfortable. New and soon-to-be parents often find choosing a baby carrier confusing given the dozens of options out there. Some are for wearing your baby facing out, some are for facing in; some are for carrying the baby on your back, while some only work for carrying the baby on the front. Some are great for newborns, while others are best for bigger tots. . . . You get the idea.

You might start your baby carrier research with a little reading. TheBabyWearer.com is an essential resource for all things babywearing. There you'll find everything from reviews to how-tos. ThePortableBaby.com has a fabulous chart that compares major brands and models to help you find the best one for you (www.theportablebaby.com/carrierfeatures.html). You'll also find lots of videos to show you how the carriers function on YouTube.com.

One of the best ways to begin to get a feel for what might be right for you is to see what other parents are wearing. On the other hand, since parents and babies come in all shapes and sizes, what works for others might not do for you at all. The best way to choose a carrier is to try wearing them with an actual baby inside.

As with so many baby products, you'll also want to think about how and when you'll use the carrier. Housework? Shopping? Errands? There are even carriers you can use in the pool! Some retailers, like PaxBaby.com, allow you to rent carriers so that you can try them in real life.

Reader Tips

Readers sound off on choosing a carrier:

Go to a baby consignment shop, where everything has been opened and you can try the carriers on. Find one that seems comfortable, and stick your kiddo in there and try shopping around for half an hour. Not all carriers will work for any given mama or baby, but it takes both of you wearing it awhile to see if it will work.

—Stephanie

My advice to parents is to figure out what baby might like best if you can—facing in, out, and so on—before purchasing an expensive carrier.

—Kara

If you can find a local babywearing group, they are an invaluable source of information. You can try on different carriers, discuss options, and get tons of information. It's a nice way to get to try a bunch of different carriers before you commit to a purchase!!

—Megan

What to Look for in a Carrier

Choose a carrier that's washable, comfortable for both parent and baby, and easy to get on and off (expect some carriers to have a learning curve). You'll also want to make sure that the carrier's fabric is seasonally or regionally appropriate. A microfleece sling's not the thing if you live in Phoenix.

The carrier should distribute the baby's weight across your body. Your shoulders shouldn't bear all of the baby's weight. Often, the lower on your body the baby's weight rests, the more comfortable you'll be.

Money-wise, it's also a good idea to invest in a carrier that will work for babies of different ages. Some types of carriers, like pouches, are best for small infants. Once baby reaches a certain size and weight, you'll find yourself shopping again.

Types of Carriers

Now for a quick rundown of the major types of baby carriers and slings:

- **Pouches** (for example, New Native). A continuous loop of fabric, pouch carriers are worn diagonally across the body. They fold up small for easy storage and transport. Since your shoulder bears much of the weight, these are best for smaller babies.
- **Ring slings** (for example, Maya Wrap). Ring slings consist of two metal rings and a long piece of fabric. Worn diagonally across the body, ring slings adjust to fit, are easy to put on, and allow for discreet breast-feeding. They're affordable, too. Suitable for newborns. Toddlers can be worn on the back with a ring sling.
- **Asian soft carriers** (for example, BabyHawk Mei Tai). The most basic kind of Mei Tai is a square of fabric with four straps that tie around the parent's body. The straps are usually padded. Because it ties,

this type of carrier can be easily adjusted to fit both parents. Can be used with newborns.

- **Soft-structured carriers** (for example, ERGObaby). A soft-structured carrier is an Asian soft carrier whose straps have quick-release buckles. The straps are usually adjustable and padded as well. Best for babies fifteen pounds and up.
- **Wrap** (for example, Moby Wrap). Wrap carriers are a great choice for newborns and smaller babies. Made from a long strip of fabrics, wraps are comfortable to wear and fit parents of a variety of sizes.

Readers' Favorite Carriers

More than a thousand Baby Cheapskate readers responded to a poll asking about their favorite baby carrier. Here are the three most popular carriers according to that poll:

- **Beco Butterfly II.** Soft-structured carrier. Can be worn on the front or back. Holds up to forty-five pounds. Includes infant insert for babies seven to fifteen pounds, allowing for use by newborns. Made from organic cotton. Some parents complain that it takes a while to learn to put this carrier on due to its complicated design. Around $140.
- **ERGObaby Original Carrier.** Soft-structured carrier. Holds up to forty pounds. Although there's an

infant insert available, ERGO is best for babies six months and up and toddlers. Can be worn on the front or back. Some petite moms complain that the ERGO is too big for their frames. The Sport version is cooler in warm weather. $115 to $145. Find it on sale for slightly less than $100.

- **Moby Wrap.** Stretchy wrap made from a wide piece of machine-washable cotton fabric. Holds newborns through babies weighing thirty-five pounds. The Moby boasts several carrying positions and works for parents of many sizes and shapes. Can take a few tries to learn to put on. Around $40.
- **BabyBjörn.** Front carrier. Holds babies eight to twenty-two pounds. If you're unfamiliar with baby-wearing, the BabyBjörn may be the first (and perhaps only) carrier that comes to mind. It's popular, but many complain about back pain since the baby's weight is carried on the shoulders and upper back. Some parents like them, though. $50 to $60. Easy to find at consignment shops.

Saving on Baby Carriers

Baby carriers can cost from $40 to $140. I mentioned making your own Moby-style wrap. What else can you do to save money on baby carriers? For starters, they're a great item for your registry.

Find bargains on gently used carriers at FrogMama .com. Enjoy free shipping, too. The online retailer Dainty Baby.com often sells returned carriers for 25 percent off or so, too. The "For Sale or Trade" forum at TheBaby Wearer.com is a great place to score a deal on a second-hand carrier, complete with photos and buyer feedback. Keep an eye on your local Craigslist board for secondhand carriers as well.

ERGObaby Carriers sometimes show up on daily deal sites like BabySteals.com and flash-sale sites at up to 50 percent off. As you might expect, they sell out quickly. Sign up for newsletters and watch these sites' Facebook pages for hints about when they'll be posting sales.

Some new carriers are easier to find on sale than others. Select manufacturers, like ERGObaby, restrict discounts on their products with MAP pricing, which I told you about earlier. To get around the restrictions, look for a storewide coupon that doesn't exclude the carrier brand. We've also seen retailers offer rebates on carriers. Just make sure the store you buy your wrap from has a great return policy in case you decide the carrier won't work for you.

Budget Mei Tai

Looking for a Mei Tai–style carrier that's easy on the budget? The Infantino Eco Sash Wrap & Tie Soft Baby Carrier is a Mei Tai–style carrier that you can pick up for less than $50. It gets good reviews, too!

TAKE IT A STEP FURTHER: Got five minutes? Make your own Moby-style wrap carrier from five to six yards of fabric. It can cost you up to 75 percent less than buying a Moby in-store, and there's no sewing required! You'll find a tutorial at www.wearyourbaby.com/Default.aspx?tabid=121.

Sling Safety

The Consumer Product Safety Commission issued safety guidelines for slings in 2010 because a dozen babies have suffocated in the past twenty years due to improper use of slings. Those guidelines can be found at the CPSC Web site (www.cpsc.gov). They include making sure you can see your baby's face when she's in the sling and making sure the baby's face isn't pressed against the sling's fabric or the parent's body.

What About Winter? Staying Warm

What do you do when it's thirty degrees outside and you want to wear your baby? You can't just put on your parka with a baby strapped to your back or chest. How do you make sure both of you are warm enough? You can buy carrier covers and ponchos, like the Peekaru Original ($80), that are made specifically for babywearing. There are less-expensive options, however. You may be able to wear the carrier *over* your coat. Dress your baby for the weather, and you both should stay toasty. If you're wearing the baby on your front in a wrap, you may be able to wear your regular winter coat. The carrier and your body heat will provide some warmth.

Reader Tip

I borrowed my husband's stretchy fleece zip-up jacket. It was stretchy enough to go around me and our son and it kept us nice and warm. On days when it was really cold, I would wear a sweatshirt underneath, put a sweatshirt on our son, and then wrap a blanket around him in the Moby or ERGO. Then I'd put the fleece jacket over the top. It kept us both toasty even during visits to Oregon's windy coast.

—Heather

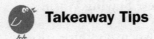

Takeaway Tips

- When choosing a stroller, consider your lifestyle as well as your budget.
- You may be able to save by buying your stroller and infant car seat in a travel system.
- There are lots of baby carriers out there—one to fit every parent and lifestyle.
- Be sure to follow safety guidelines when using a carrier.
- Save by looking for a secondhand stroller or carrier or snag a deal on a daily deal or flash-sale site.

Chapter 13

• • •

Gearing Up: Bouncers, Bassinets, and More

Sometimes new parents can feel like a particular piece of baby gear is all that stands between them and the loony bin. In my case it was the baby swing. I'll always remember it as "the machine that will make the baby stop crying so I can get a few minutes of sleep." Many—and I do mean many—a wee hour of the morning was spent cranking that thing up as high as it would go in hopes that my fussy but loveable kid would finally conk out. Sometimes I'd have to leave it on high all night, hoping the batteries didn't run out while I was (finally!) asleep. That thing ate up D batteries like they were Twinkies, too. I always made sure I had a stockpile of them.

Of course, with the passage of time comes perspective. I realize now that even more beneficial to my sanity than the baby swing would have been trusting my ability as a parent to soothe my child rather than putting all my faith in a piece of baby gear. I didn't *need* the swing; I needed sleep and my overtired baby needed sleep. The swing was a tool that helped me meet those needs more conveniently. That's what every piece of baby gear really is—a tool. Not a single swing, bouncer, play yard, or jumper has any magic powers. They're conveniences that—if we're lucky—will make taking care of a baby easier and more fun.

Some baby gear takes up a lot more space than it's worth. It can be expensive, too. To improve your return on investment it's important to consider both your lifestyle and your living space when you think about what baby gear you might like to bring into your home. Some of what's out there will fit right into both. Some won't.

The array of baby gadgets available to parents is staggering. This chapter will focus on a few tried-and-true "baby entertainers" and show parents how to find great deals on them. We'll also discuss nap-time gear—play yards, cradles, bassinets, and Moses baskets.

A Play Yard Playbook

Are play yards a must-have? I posed that question to readers at the Baby Cheapskate Facebook page: whether they thought play yards were necessary. As with so many other baby products, some said that they were an essential for every parent, while others said that they hardly used theirs.

Some had skipped them altogether and hadn't missed them. We can gather with absolute certainty that some parents will find them essential while others won't (*wink*).

Your lifestyle determines how helpful you'll find a play yard. Parents with large homes and parents who travel find them the handiest. Moms and dads with two-story homes often set them up downstairs as convenient diaper changing and napping stations, while on-the-go families take their play yards along on their travels as portable cribs. Other parents like having the play yard in their master bedrooms so that their newborns can sleep close by. Ironically, most babies don't seem to spend much time in play yards actually playing.

Your baby will get the most use out of a play yard before he's a year old, though some continue to nap in them until they're about two, or until they reach the weight and/ or height limit given for the particular model (usually around thirty pounds and thirty-five inches tall). The bassinet that comes with some play yards, of course, won't serve you nearly as long. Most max out at around fifteen pounds. Changing stations can usually hold toddlers up to about twenty-five pounds.

Reader Tips

Readers share how they used their play yards:

We used our Pack 'n Play during the first few months of our baby's life when she slept in the room with us. It was great as a changing table and bassinet until we were ready to move her to the crib.

—Bethany

We keep it at my in-laws' for when they watch her.

—Jessica

I have twins, so I kept one downstairs and used the changing table feature. It was nice because I could then keep a good stock of diapers, wipes, and outfits in the Pack 'n Play instead of running upstairs every time I needed something.

—Darleen

I got one with all the bells and whistles for about $90 by Graco. I could have saved $40 or so by buying the standard one. I never used the changing part or the mobile. We mostly used it on trips.

—Emily

When my kiddos were newborns we kept it in our living room for quick naps and diaper changes since all our bedrooms were on a different floor.

—Karen

I used one with both of my girls as their "crib" because we didn't want to get a real crib since babies rarely sleep in there anyways and they're so expensive.

—Vi

We use it primarily when we go outside to play. That way the baby can have a safe place to play and I don't have to worry about him eating whatever he finds on the ground. Of course, it also serves well as a good travel bed.

—Rebeca

Shopping

There are dozens and dozens of play yards on the market, costing anywhere from $50 to $250 or more. Amazon alone carries more than forty models. Prices differ according to brand, fabric, and features. My best advice, naturally, is to spend as little as possible.

You can save big by picking up a secondhand play yard, but keep in mind that play yards are often recalled. Check for recalls at CPSC.gov before buying and inspect the play yard carefully.

If you buy new, there's no reason to spend more than about $85 for a play yard with a bassinet or more than $100 for one with both a bassinet and a changer. There are dozens of different features to entice you to spend more than that, including rotating canopies, folding feet, diaper stackers, built-in nightlights, and vibration. Skip all the bells and whistles—especially the ones that require batteries. You don't need them.

What to Look For

Honestly? I just can't get too excited about any particular play yard models. If you look beyond the gadgets, there's very little difference between them. Choose your play yard by whether or not it will meet the requirements of the use you have in mind for it.

If your primary use for the play yard is travel, look for a lightweight, easy-to-set-up model with a sturdy carry bag and skip the bassinet and changing station. Or save yourself fifteen pounds and go for the PeaPod travel bed. The Graco Travel Lite Crib weighs in at under twenty pounds. You can find it for under $70 on sale.

If you plan to use the play yard as a mini nursery in your home, get one with the bassinet and/or the changing station attachments and with tons of pockets for all your necessities. Beyond that, you may as well choose one that looks pretty or matches your decor.

Parents I've talked to are big fans of Graco Pack 'n Play play yards. They earn great reviews online, too. You can easily pick up one with a bassinet and/or changing station for under $70. Safety 1st and Baby Trend make nice play yards for around $90. All three brands go on sale frequently.

$ QUICK AND EASY SAVINGS $

If you're willing to forgo the bassinet and changing table, you can pick up a play yard for about $50. The Cosco Funsport gets great reviews. You can find it for about that price at Target, Walmart, or Amazon.

Will Your Baby Be a Swinger or a Bouncer?

Sure, swings and bouncers can keep your baby entertained, but they can do so much more. As I mentioned earlier, our swing turned out to be an invaluable baby soother. The bouncer, for me, was a place to put the baby down for a few minutes while I took a shower, got some lunch, and so on.

What's funny about these two popular pieces of baby gear is that babies tend to have a very clear preference for one over the other. A while ago I posted a poll asking readers to tell me whether a swing or a bouncer soothed their babies more. Nearly two thousand readers responded: 43 percent of babies preferred the swing, 27 percent preferred the bouncer, and less than a quarter of the babies in question were soothed by both the bouncer *and* the swing; 6 percent didn't like either one.

That's why it's important to be careful with your swing and/or bouncer purchases. Above all, if you're buying new, wait for a great sale (try to save at least 35 percent) and buy from a store with a generous return policy. Following are a few features and models to look for.

What to Look for in a Swing

Most swings come with a three-point restraint system, washable seat pad, nonslip feet, at least two reclining positions, and at least five speeds. Some of them also feature music, vibration, lights, a toy bar, and more. Look for a swing that has a timer and that operates quietly—you don't want a lot of squeaking or thumping when your baby's trying to fall asleep. You'll also want one that lets you control the volume of the music it plays. It's a handy feature that can preserve your sanity as well as soothe your baby.

If you're short on space, or plan to take your swing with you anywhere, look for a portable swing. While not as powerful as full-sized swings, portable swings are less expensive and take up less space than their full-sized counterparts.

One reason for opting for a full-sized swing is that some of them plug into the wall, eliminating the need for batteries (the choice will cost you, though). Some full-sized swings also have a slightly higher weight limit, allowing for longer use.

Some full-sized swings move in the traditional front-to-back pattern, while others can also move from side to side (like a baby in a cradle). Because the baby lies down to swing with this type rather than using it more vertically, cradle-style swings are only good until your baby wants to sit up.

5 Swing Picks

Bright Starts is known for budget-friendly baby gear. Their Comfort & Harmony Portable Swing lists for around $60, and is easy to find on sale for less than $50. It holds up to twenty-five pounds, and requires four C batteries.

The Fisher-Price Take Along Swing retails for $50 to $70, and is also easy to find on sale. It also holds up to twenty-five pounds and requires four C batteries.

When it comes to full-sized swings, readers love the Fisher-Price Open-Top Cradle Swing, the Graco Lovin' Hug Swing, and the Fisher-Price Cradle Swing. All three can easily be found for less than $100 on sale.

What to Look for in a Bouncer

Bouncers are handy places for baby to both nap and play. Luckily, bouncers tend to be a bit cheaper than swings. It's easy to find them for less than $50. Look for good bouncing action, nonskid feet, a washable seat pad, and a three-point restraint system. Bouncers can also feature music, vibration, flashing lights, and toy bars. *Whoo-hoo!*

If you're a minimalist, you'll be happy to know that

there are some stylish gadget-free (and battery-free) bouncers on the market. Rather than getting what you pay for with these bouncers, though, you pay for what you *don't* get. Stylish bouncers from Maclaren, BabyBjörn, and others can run $100 or more.

Bouncer Picks

- The Infantino Fold and Go Bouncer lists for about $50. It needs three AAA batteries and folds up for easy transport.
- Fisher-Price Bouncers range from $35 to $60 and hold up to twenty-five pounds. They require four D batteries.
- Tiny Love Gymini Bouncer is also about $50. One lithium metal battery required.

Swing and Bouncer Shopping Tips

So how do you buy for baby without knowing which will tickle your baby's fancy? The truth is, there's really no way to predict whether your child will prefer a swing or a bouncer. You just have to wait and see.

You'll save the most dough, of course, by doing without both types of electronic soothers and relying on pure parent power. Not an option? Well, you can always buy both, budget permitting, but chances are your baby won't like one or the other, and one of your pricey purchases will gather dust in the corner. That's why it makes so much sense to try to borrow a bouncer and/or swing from friends until you figure out which, if either, your child prefers.

Another thing many expectant parents don't realize is that most babies will only use a bouncer or swing until they're about twenty-five pounds (around a year old for many babies) and will probably *enjoy* using it for only a few weeks. Since swings and bouncers are used for such a limited amount of time, there's generally plenty of life left in them when parents pass them on.

If you can't score a bouncer and/or swing for free via a generous friend or Freecycle, try to find a gently used one at your local kiddie consignment shop, on Craigslist, or at a yard sale or consignment sale. A quick check of my local Craigslist board today reveals full-sized swings for $35, a bouncer for $12, and more.

For brand-new swings and bouncers, try the Web site NoBetterDeal.com for big discounts on open-box items. If you don't have any luck, then check the usual discount retailers—Amazon, Target, and Walmart—for sales. I like Amazon for online shopping because they offer free shipping and free returns if you end up not liking what you buy. A quick check of Amazon today reveals the popular Fisher-Price Rainforest Cradle Swing for 32 percent off and a matching bouncer for 29 percent off. Or shop in-store and you can check out the features and performance of floor models. You can get lucky sometimes at Babies"R"Us and find open-box items for less.

$ QUICK AND EASY SAVINGS $

Want a new swing or bouncer as opposed to used? Check the Web site NoBetterDeal.com for open-box swings, bouncers, and other baby gear items. NBD has a great reputation with readers and a reasonable shipping policy.

TAKE IT A STEP FURTHER: You'll be done with most of the baby gear items discussed in this chapter in a few months. If you won't be saving it for subsequent kids, resell your gently used baby gear to help recoup the cost.

Rock On, Baby: Rockers

One of the most popular baby entertainers on the market right now isn't a bouncer or swing at all. It's a rocker. Baby rockers serve the same function as bouncers—play place and napping nook. There are two main players in this gear category:

- Fisher-Price Newborn Rock 'n Play Sleeper. The Rock 'n Play is a favorite with parents that babies can use from day one. List price is about $60, and it's easy to find on sale for less. Some parents use this as a travel bed. Its maximum weight is twenty-five pounds.

- The hugely popular Fisher-Price Infant to Toddler Rocker has a bit more staying power. Listing for about $40, this infant seat morphs into a toddler rocker that will hold up to forty pounds. It requires one D Battery.

Bassinets, Cradles, and Moses Baskets

Bassinets, cradles, and cosleepers function as mini cribs. Some parents like to put them in their bedrooms before their babies are ready to sleep in their cribs. Cradles rock, and some bassinets do, too. Some bassinets have wheels so that they can easily be moved from room to room, and some feature music and other soothing sounds. If you're considering a used or heirloom bassinet or cradle, check carefully to make sure it meets current safety guidelines.

Moses baskets are woven baskets with handles used by napping infants. They come with a mattress or padding. Most have handles for carrying—though for safety reasons you're not supposed to pick them up with baby inside them.

The drawbacks to bassinets, cradles, and Moses baskets are that they are often outgrown in less than three months (most can be used only until baby weighs around fifteen pounds), and that you'll need special sheets for them (which will also be quickly outgrown). Considering that most bassinets cost over $100 and most Moses baskets cost $40 or more, I suggest skipping them in favor of a play yard, which has a longer useful life.

Bumbo and BébéPOD: A Different Kind of Babysitter

The Bumbo Baby Sitter is a soft foam chair that allows your baby to hang out in a sitting position as soon as she can hold her head steady, but before she can actually sit up. The seat has a twenty-two-pound weight limit and lists for a pricey $40 or so. A tray is sold separately. BébéPOD, made by Prince Lionheart, is a popular competitor to Bumbo and costs about the same. The bébéPOD comes with the tray, however.

Reader Tips

Bumbo was a great way to keep my daughter entertained while I took a shower or cooked dinner. I used it just at those times with the activity mat. Seeing it from a different angle made it seem like a new toy and gave me precious moments of peace and quiet!

—Carrie

Neither of my babies cared for the Bumbo and they would usually end up slouched over to one side. They seemed to be happier if I just put them in the high chair and moved it into the kitchen (or wherever I wanted to be).

—Kristy

Some babies like these products and the new perspective on things they offer, and some despise them. Babies with chubby thighs can get stuck, and I've read several reports of babies arching their backs and falling out. For safety's sake, use a Bumbo on the floor only—no tabletops or other high surfaces.

If you want to try the Bumbo or bébéPOD, it's smart not to pay full price. Check consignment stores and other secondhand sources. At the time of this writing, my local Craigslist board had several Bumbos and bébéPODs for $15 to $20.

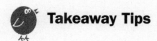 **Takeaway Tips**

- Whether your baby will get a lot of use out of a play yard depends on your lifestyle, your home's layout, and other variables.
- A play yard can double as a satellite nursery if you have a two-story home.
- Few babies like both bouncers *and* swings. Try to learn which your baby prefers before purchasing or save by buying secondhand.
- Swings and bouncers have a weight limit. Don't over-

spend on items you'll only use for a few months at most.

- Swings can burn through batteries. If that concerns you, look for a full-sized model that plugs into the wall.
- Rockers can serve as play space and napping space as well. They're increasingly popular alternatives to bouncers.

Chapter 14

• • •

Choosing Drool-worthy First Toys

My son is six years old now. We try to keep the TV tuned to PBS when he watches it, but there are a couple of shows on another network that he really likes. That other network has commercials. It's funny, and not just a little scary, how readily he believes that the products these commercials hawk really are as marvelous as the ads say they are. He'll watch a commercial about, say, some cheesy picture-hanging system, and then he'll come in and say to me excitedly, "Mommy, you really ought to get the [insert ridiculous product name here]. Then your pictures won't be crooked when you hang them. It's really easy to use." Sometimes he even quotes the commercials verbatim. The companies really should pay him.

My son has clearly reached the age where he tells us what toys he absolutely can't live without. Usually they're one-trick wonders with zero educational value that require half a dozen batteries so they can whistle or beep repeatedly in a headache-inducing fashion. Yippee. We know that were we to buy them he'd play with them for a week or less, tops.

It's easier with babies and toddlers, because *you* get to do the choosing when it comes to toys and other fun stuff. This chapter will show you how to choose quality entertaining items for your baby's first year of life. We're talking mobiles, crib soothers, baby gyms, entertainment centers, rattles, blocks, and more with proven staying power.

How many toys does a parent *need* to buy for a new baby? Zero. Zip. Nada. Newborns can't hold their heads up, much less shake a rattle (a fact that surprised me as a new parent for some reason). In fact, babies aren't really interested in playing with toys for the first few months. Until they can sit up, babies are all about looking and listening to the world around them and trying to figure out what this crazy planet is all about.

Of course, that doesn't mean babies don't like to have fun. Entertainment, for young babies, consists simply of a bit of visual and auditory stimulation. Mobiles, mirrors, and other crib toys come to mind. But there's one thing they get a kick out of more than anything else, and that's you. That's right. *You.*

Baby will love nothing more than staring at your face and listening to your voice—even if you haven't had time to shower or brush your teeth. Why else would she think a game of peekaboo with Mom or Dad is so awesome? Of course, you can't be the star of the show 100 percent of the time no matter how much your little one would love that. You'll probably want to give your baby something entertaining to look at and/or listen to. Here are a few suggestions:

- Hang a nursery mobile above the crib or changing table (see chapter 5 for more on mobiles).
- Unbreakable mirrors like those made by Sassy are another great choice. She'll be fascinated by the other baby looking back at her—she won't understand that it's her own face for quite a while. Most of these mirrors can also be used on the floor for tummy time.
- Fisher-Price crib soothers are also a popular choice. They hang on the side of the crib and entertain baby with bubbles, moving figures, and soothing music. The Fisher-Price soothers are available in several varieties to match most of Fisher-Price's popular lines of baby gear.

> **TAKE IT A STEP FURTHER: MAKE YOUR OWN BABY GYM** Got more time on your hands than money? There are several tutorials online that show you how to make your own baby gym. For starters, check out the one at thepaisleycupcake.blogspot .com/2010/06/baby-activity-mat.html.

Tummy-time Fun: Activity Mats and Baby Gyms

Activity mats, aka baby gyms, are colorful, washable, padded mats that you lay your baby on for fun or "tummy time." Most activity mats have a bar or two of themed toys that hangs overhead, and there's usually some music involved. They're often the first "toy" a baby enjoys, since there's no gripping involved—just staring, batting, and kicking. Most activity mats are quite portable and come with a carry bag.

Activity mats can cost anywhere from $10 to around $110. Major manufacturers include Fisher-Price, Tiny Love, Infantino, and Graco (sold under the Baby Einstein label). Bright Starts makes one for around $25 on sale. They're easily found at consignment stores and sales, too.

Babies usually enjoy using a baby gym until they're ready to sit up, though some continue to play with theirs until they crawl. Look for a baby gym that has detachable toys and you'll get a little more life out of it.

Classic First Toys Your Baby Will Go Gaga For

Once baby can reach out and grasp items, he's ready for toys like rattles, teethers, and cloth books. Look for toys with lots of textures and colors and toys that rattle, crinkle, or jingle. Once they're at this stage, everything goes straight to the mouth, so make sure whatever he's playing with is drool-proof and washable (either in the dishwasher or in the washing machine). Also, pay attention to age guidelines. They're based on developmental stages. If your baby's not there yet, the toy is bound to be a dud, or worse, dangerous.

You know who's going to be playing with baby toys the most? You. Don't expect a baby to play with a toy on his or her own. Expect to participate and guide play. Show your baby how to play with the toy.

Saving Money on Baby Toys

It's easy-peasy to save on baby toys. Here are a few ideas:

- Repurpose what you have. Babies' favorite "toys" can be things you already have around the house. Let baby practice stacking and nesting with measuring cups, plastic drinking cups, or empty boxes.
- Because toys for babies are used for a fairly short amount of time, they usually don't suffer much wear and tear. You should have no problem finding gently used infant toys at your local kiddie consignment shop or other secondhand source. Since these toys will likely be out of the package, check them carefully for safety and look them up online to check for age appropriateness and recalls.

- Host a toy swap. As anybody who's attended a baby playdate knows, the best toy is the one the other kid is playing with.
- Buy at the holidays for big savings. From Black Friday (the day after Thanksgiving) through the week before Christmas, you can save up to 50 percent on toys at retailers both online and off.

Reader Tip

Of all things his favorite "toy" was the ceiling fan. He would coo and get all excited every time we would lay him under it.

—Jackie

Most-loved Toys for Babies Five Months to Twelve Months

Babies have different personalities. What makes one baby coo and giggle may make another burst into tears. There are thousands of baby toys on the market, so how do you spend wisely on the good ones? Turn to the wisdom of the masses, of course.

In truth, there's no one toy that every kid likes, but the eight toys on the list below have proven track records. Hundreds of Baby Cheapskate readers have responded to more than half a dozen polls posted thrice yearly over several years about which toys babies loved playing with and *kept* playing with for a long time. I compiled this list of most-loved toys for the under-one set from their responses. It's not just Baby Cheapskate readers that love these toys, though. Many of them are award winners. Look for them on Amazon and other Web sites and you'll find dozens—sometimes hundreds—of great ratings from shoppers.

What else do the toys on the list have in common? They all familiarize babies with numbers, letters, colors, and shapes, and encourage them to develop their motor skills. Oh, and they all require batteries, unfortunately. Look them up online to learn more when you're ready to bring some toys into your home. Watch for sales on these toys at stores like Amazon, Target, and Walmart.

- **Playskool Busy Ball Popper.** Balls roll down a track and pop up as music plays. Nine months and up. Around $20 on sale.
- **Fisher-Price Laugh & Learn Learning Kitchen.** Features food-shaped blocks, music, and cooking sounds. In English and Spanish. Six months and up. Around $30 on sale.
- **Fisher-Price Laugh & Learn Learning Home.** ABCs, 123s, twenty-one sing-along songs, and more. Six months and up. Around $80 on sale.
- **Fisher-Price Laugh & Learn Fun with Friends Table.** Encourages standing. Like the other Laugh &

Learn toys, the table features ABCs, 123s, music, opposites, and more. Six months and up. Around $40 on sale.

- **LeapFrog Learn and Groove Table.** Similar to the Laugh & Learn table, the LeapFrog table features more than forty sounds, real musical instrument sounds, and more. Two modes of play: learning mode and music mode. Spanish and English. Six months and up. Around $37 on sale.
- **Munchkin Mozart Magic Cube.** Features Mozart masterpieces. Babies can add or subtract instruments to the melodies. All ages. Around $19 on sale.
- **Fisher-Price Stride-to-Ride Lion.** Starts out as a walker and converts to a ride-on toy. Features music, lights, and lion sounds. Nine months and up. Around $37 on sale.
- **LeapFrog My Pal Scout/Violet.** Touch the paws of plush Scout (or his gal pal, Violet) and hear learning tunes about colors, shapes, animals, and more. Six months and up. Around $20 on sale.

In addition to these toys, pre-toddlers love teethers, stacking blocks and cups, and shape sorters. The list below lists specific toys of this type that were a hit with readers' kids.

Drool-worthy Teethers

Teething babies love nothing more than chewing on whatever's handiest. Give them something safe to gnaw on and everybody's the better for it. I asked Baby Cheapskate readers to share their picks for best baby teethers, and these BPA-free faves made the list:

- **Vulli's Sophie the Giraffe.** Hugely popular Sophie was the bestselling baby item at Amazon at the time of this writing. Mademoiselle is made from natural rubber and painted with food-grade paint. She's pricey, though, at around $18 on sale. Vulli's Chan Pie Gnon is similar, and costs a bit less.
- **Philips AVENT Range BPA-Free Front Teeth Teether.** This simple ring-shaped teether is easy to grab and nicely priced. Around $5.50 on sale.
- **Manhattan Toy Winkel.** Made from colorful loops of pliable plastic. Around $11 on sale.
- **HABA Kringelring.** Eco-friendly teether made from beechwood and maple parts strung together in a ring on an elastic band. Around $9 on sale.
- **RaZbaby RaZ-Berry Teether.** A nubby silicone binky. Around $5 on sale.
- **Lifefactory Multi-Sensory Silicone Teether.** A lightweight silicone ring with several different textures. Around $6.99.

Rattles

Check out this list of readers' kids' favorite rattles. When you're in the market, be sure to give these a fair shake.

- **Sassy Rattlin Rings.** Eight textured plastic links on a ring. Kind of like your car keys, and we all know how babies love keys. Top-rack dishwasher safe. Around $3.50 on sale.
- **Lamaze Mortimer the Moose.** Mortimer's parts crinkle, rattle, and crunch. He's also got a clip on top for attaching to a stroller, diaper bag, and so on. Oh, and he's cuddly, too. Around $12 on sale.
- **Bright Starts Rattle and Shake Barbell Rattle.** A classic barbell-shaped rattle with clear ends filled with colorful beads and a mirror. Nicely priced at about $2.99.
- **Lamaze Jacques the Peacock.** Bestselling Jacques features crinkly, textured tail feathers, a squeaker, and a mirror. The clip on top lets you attach him to a stroller, diaper bag, and so on. Around $11 on sale.

Best Shape Sorters: 4 Picks

Shape sorters help babies learn to recognize shapes and develop hand-eye coordination. They're a great "first toy" for babies, and should see peak usage from about six months to about eighteen months. Here are Baby Cheap-skate readers' top four picks:

- **Fisher-Price Brilliant Basics Baby's First Blocks.** It's super-simple, and offers built-in storage for blocks. Around $8 on sale.
- **Tupperware Shape O.** Another one you may have played with as a kid. It rolls with a rattling sound. Several readers played with this when *they* were kids. That's some staying power! $17.50 at Tupperware .com.
- **Infantino Barn Shape Sorter.** Not just a shape sorter, this toy has spin and slide beads, a clock, and more. Shape-sorting letters encourage letter recognition. Around $13 on sale.
- **Melissa & Doug Wooden Shape Sorting Clock.** This toy has long been a favorite of Baby Cheap-skate readers. It's fun for babies, and can be used later to help kids learn to tell time. Around $12 on sale.

Stacking and Sorting Toys

Stacking and nesting toys help babies and toddlers learn about spatial relationships and help them improve hand-eye coordination. Here are my top seven, based on reader feedback, sales, reviews, and a little personal experience:

- **Fisher-Price Rock-a-Stack.** It doesn't get any more classic than this, folks. Around $7.50 on sale.
- **Fisher-Price Little Superstar Classical Stacker.** Take the Rock-a-Stack and add a few bells and whistles. Around $15 on sale.
- **Green Toys My First Stacker.** Winner of the 2010 Oppenheim Gold Award. Made from recycled plastic. Around $11 on sale.
- **Fisher-Price Brilliant Basics Stack & Roll Cups.** Each brightly colored cup has a different texture. Around $11 on sale.
- **eeBoo Tot Towers Nesting Blocks.** Graduated boxes for stacking and nesting. Around $19 on sale.
- **MULA Stack n Nest Cups.** Interesting patterns and shapes. A steal at under $3 at IKEA.
- **Especially for Baby Stacking Cups from Babies"R"Us.** Simple, inexpensive, and portable. Nicely priced at around $4.

Stationary Activity Centers:
Plastic Mega Hunks of Fun

Stationary activity centers are commonly referred to as ExerSaucers, though the word "ExerSaucer" is kind of like the word "Kleenex," a brand name that came to stand in for a whole class of products. "ExerSaucer" really refers to stationary activity centers made by Evenflo. Occasionally, you'll also hear the terms "discovery center," "activity saucer," "entertainer," and "activity station." Besides Evenflo, you'll find activity centers by Graco (under the name Baby Einstein), Bright Starts, and others.

Many pre-crawling babies get a kick out of activity centers from about four months through a year, with the peak age of about six months. Some find them seriously overstimulating, however, so consider your child's temperament before buying.

Stationary activity centers look like those walkers that we used to have when we were kids (those are now frowned upon), but without wheels. Most also allow your tot to rock, spin, and bounce in one place and play with a variety of toys. Most also feature music and sounds, too.

The downside of activity centers is that they are big, bulky, gaudy hunks of plastic (around thirty inches in diameter) that take up a large part of whatever room they're placed in. They can run through batteries like nobody's business—one model takes a whopping nine AAAs. They can be pricey, too.

New activity centers start at around $40 and top out at over $100. Luckily, they're pretty easy to find secondhand. When buying secondhand, inspect the activity center carefully for safety and check for recalls before buying. Make sure you have access to the product instructions. If the booklet isn't there, you may be able to download one at the manufacturer's Web site or have one mailed to you by calling the manufacturer.

Shopping Tips

Start researching activity centers online, where you can read lots of reviews to see what other parents loved and hated about particular models. Check the manufacturers' Web sites to see if replacement toys are available in case one should break.

Features to Consider

- Does the activity center feature music or sounds? A volume control can be a sanity saver for parents.
- An activity center with several height settings will allow for longer use.
- Those that can spin 360 degrees will allow your curious tot to keep tabs on what the rest of the family is up to.
- The body of the activity center should disassemble for easy cleaning, and the toys should be washable. The seat pad should be easily removable and machine washable.
- Look for stabilizers so that you can control the bounce if your baby's not into it.
- If you're short on space, find one that will fold for storage. A carry handle is, well, handy, too.
- Choose one that's battery-free or only takes a couple of AAAs to avoid feeling like you should have bought stock in Duracell.

After you've narrowed down your list to a few candidates, it's time to head to a local retailer or consignment store to give the floor models a whirl. Tug on attached toys. They shouldn't come out too easily. Check to see if it spins smoothly and how easy it is to bounce. The whole thing should feel sturdy. If it's a folding model, see if it folds easily and smoothly. When you find something you like, use your smartphone to see whether you can beat the price by buying online.

Bouncing Baby Boys and Girls: Jumpers

Stationary jumpers are a very popular alternative to the activity center and a safer alternative to those springy contraptions that hang from the doorway. The Jumperoo by Fisher-Price features a spinning seat, lights, music, and other sounds and folds for easy transport. It requires three AAA batteries. The Jumperoo lists for $90 or so, but with a little sale scouting you should be able to find one for $75 or so. Check your favorite secondhand sources to score one for even less.

Pay special attention to the height limits for these toys. Kids who are too tall can flip them over. When your child can walk (or even stand up), it's time to put away the activity center or stationary jumper.

Reader Tips

Readers sound off on activity centers:

My son loved it. It was great to have a safe place for him so I could get things done at home, plus it had the added benefit of making him poop within fifteen minutes of being put in there!

—Laura

My daughter . . . didn't like to be contained in anything! She would be content for five to ten minutes in it. Same with the jumper and walker and swing! I am glad we were able to borrow all our baby gear like this . . . and didn't waste our money buying one 'cause they didn't get much use!

—Heather

We had a Jumperoo at home, and an ExerSaucer that he used at day care. He loved the Jumperoo, but was only okay in the ExerSaucer. He would play, but never for very long, and would try to make it bounce more than it was meant to (like the Jumperoo did).

—Susan

Books, Music, and Other Media
for Your Little Mogul

Books

Reading with your baby is a great way to play together, no matter how young she is! As you read and look at pictures together she'll build vocabulary and start to understand how language sounds work.

Saving on board books is really easy. We were given dozens of hand-me-down board books for free. Many libraries carry board books, too. Ours always had a big basketful in the children's section. Search the posts at your local Freecycle for free board books, too.

I asked Baby Cheapskate readers how they built their board book libraries for cheap. Answers ranged from Goodwill to garage sales to Grandma. eBay.com is also worth checking. I found a lot of gently used books for just over a buck each on eBay. Just be sure to factor in shipping to your overall cost.

Cleaning secondhand board books is a snap. Most board books are washable or have laminated pages that can be wiped down with disinfecting wipes or a little alcohol. If you want new books, stores like T.J.Maxx, Marshalls, and Ross carry them for 30 to 50 percent off the cover price.

Smart Idea: Have a Board Book Baby Shower

Are you one of the lucky ones who gets to have more than one baby shower? Why not make one of them a board book shower? Each guest brings a favorite board book instead of a traditional gift.

TAKE IT A STEP FURTHER: BOOK SWAPS When your baby is ready for new additions to her library, why not host a book swap? You provide the snacks, and other parents bring gently used books they've finished with.

Reader Nicole swaps books online at PaperBackSwap .com. She posts books she's finished with and trades with others for just the cost of mailing. Nicole says it's ". . . a great resource for not only board books, but picture books and chapter books as the kiddos grow and their needs change. Good for parents, too—baby care books can be swapped out for toddler activity books and so on."

How to Save on Music for Baby

Babies adore music. Singing or humming to your baby is free, of course, and she won't even care if you're off-key.

Beyond that, you can find free or inexpensive baby music CDs at many of the same places you find bargain board books—libraries, yard sales, hand-me-downs, and more.

Reader Hillary suggests looking through what you already have to find music for baby. She says, "Our daughter's favorite CD is a disc of Hawaiian music we bought on our honeymoon; she falls asleep listening to it every day. And she loves dancing along in her car seat to the rock music we play on the radio."

There are lots of free sources of music, too. Pandora .com is a free-to-use Internet music station that lets you customize your own "channel" and play music on your computer or smartphone. Click on Pandora's "family" genre and you'll see premade stations of lullabies, toddler music, and folk songs. Want to foster a love of classical music in your little genius, too? Pandora has tons of that as well.

Useless Baby Product Alert: Baby Videos

The American Academy of Pediatrics discourages all television watching for children two and under (www.healthychildren.org). That means cartoons as well as all those "turn your baby into a genius" and reading DVDs are a no-go. Instead, says the AAP, babies and toddlers should be involved in active play.

Out and About with Bambino

And speaking of active play, new parents deserve a little F.U.N. as well. Why not pop your baby into his stroller or carrier and get out and about? It's called maternity *leave* for a reason, you know. Go for a walk! Visit with a friend! Do some window-shopping! Hang out at the playground and watch the older tots play. Getting out of the house is a great antidote to the isolation that new parents often feel. Need ideas for outings? The wonderful Web site Rookie Moms.com lists hundreds of age-appropriate free or cheap activities that new parents can do with their babies.

 Takeaway Tips

- You are your baby's favorite toy. Human interaction is way better than any fancy toy or video.
- Always buy age-appropriate toys.
- Check battery requirements before buying toys.
- Save big by buying secondhand toys and media.
- Avoid television and videos for kids two and under.
- Have fun outside the house, too.

There's another reason besides entertainment to hang out with other parents. It makes you smarter. That's what I've learned in the years since I started BabyCheapskate .com. By listening to other parents, whether you agree with their philosophy of parenting or not, you learn what's worth doing and worth buying. It's a perspective far more valuable than the paid-for parenting tips and product accolades you see in advertisements and marketing materials.

So now that you've come to the last pages of the book, you should feel savvy to marketers' tricks. You know the difference between real information and marketing and between wants and needs. You know how to find great deals on the baby items you choose to bring into your home. I want to leave you with one last thing to think about:

We parents want to ensure our babies' comfort and contentment and may be lured into buying any product that promises to deliver it. As it turns out, skipping some of those baby "must-haves" is not only better for your wallet now, but can pay off big-time for your offspring down the road.

As Pamela Paul says in *Parenting, Inc.*, "catering to every wish and whim, we teach our children that their interests should always be top priority, regardless of effort. We teach them to be less flexible about accommodating other people and we instill a sense of entitlement" [Paul, Pamela (2010-04-01). Parenting, Inc. (Kindle Locations 847-850). Times Books. Kindle Edition.]. A flexible, resourceful kid can become a flexible, resourceful adult.

Should baby get a little bored without a dozen tchotchkes strapped to her stroller she just may end up more creative as a result. When we deny kids—even very young ones—the opportunity to learn how to deal with a little discomfort, frustration, and disappointment now, we set them up for harder lessons later. Without these coping skills it's easy to imagine our kids years down the road— maybe as soon-to-be parents themselves—buying stuff for comfort, and creating a multigenerational financial headache.

So congratulations. Welcome to parenthood. Trust that despite what marketers may tell you, the real tools, resources, and know-how it takes to navigate the winding road of parenting can't be bought from any store or Web site. Trust that you have what it takes and go out there and enjoy the strange and wonderful journey. If you get a chance, stop by BabyCheapskate.com and let us know how it's going.

Appendix A
100+ Helpful Web Sites for Smart Shoppers

• • •

At Baby Cheapskate

BabyCheapskate.com

Coupon-trading group: Groups.Google.com/group/
BCCouponTraders

Facebook page: facebook.com/babycheapskate (Come
ask a question or say hi!)

Monthly deal and sale forecasts: http://bit.ly/BCPredicts

Health and Product Safety

CPSC.gov (Consumer Product Safety Commission)

GoodGuide.org

GreenGuard.org

HealthyChildren.org

Recalls.gov

SafeMama.com

Car Seat Safety and Info
Car-Safety.org
Car-Seat.org
NHTSA's Child Safety site: www.nhtsa.gov/Safety/CPS
The Car Seat Lady: thecarseatlady.wordpress.com

Free and Cheap Stuff
Craigslist.org
eBay.com
Freecycle.org
HandMeDowns.com
KidsConsignmentSales.com
ReCrib.com
SwapBabyGoods.com
SwapMamas.com
ThredUp.com

Printable Coupons
Coupons.com
Coupons.Target.com
MamboSprouts.com
ShortCuts.com
SmartSource.com

Coupon Sign-Ups
Aveeno: aveeno.com/user/register
Beech-Nut: www.beechnut.com/Special%20Offers/

Burt's Bees: hive.burtsbees.com/clients/burtsbees/survey
.htm

Earth's Best: EarthsBest.com

Enfamil Family Beginnings: www.enfamil.com

Gerber: www.gerber.com/login/register.aspx

GoodStart: www.gerber.com/login/register.aspx

HappyBaby: www.happybabyfood.com/
community/79/126-sign-in

Huggies: www.huggies.com/en-US/register

Johnson's Baby: johnsonsbaby.com/offers

Nature's Goodness (Del Monte): www.naturesgoodness
.com

Pampers: www.pampers.com/en_US/signup

Price Chopper Baby Club: www2.pricechopper.com/
babyclub/index.shtml

Publix Baby Club: www.publix.com/clubs/baby/
Subscribe.do

Save-a-Lot Being Well Baby Club: www.save-a-lot.com/
ads-promotions/promotions/being-well-baby

Seventh Generation: www.seventhgeneration.com/
coupons

ShopRite Baby Bucks: www.shoprite.com/BabyBucks
.aspx

Similac Strong Moms: www.similac.com

Sprout: www.sproutbabyfood.com

Winn-Dixie Baby Club: www.winndixie.com/Reward_
Card/Baby_Club_Program.asp

Couponing and Deal Info
AFullCup.com
HotCouponWorld.com
RetailMeNot.com
ShopLocal.com
SlickDeals.net
WeUseCoupons.com

Mobile and Location-based Coupons
Cellfire.com (also offers printable coupons)
CouponSherpa.com
Foursquare.com (get coupons delivered to your
    smartphone when you "check in" at a store that
    offers them)
GetYowza.com (smartphone app–based)
GroceryIQ.com (integrated coupons and grocery lists)
Zavers.com

Unbiased Product Reviews
Buzzillions.com
ConsumerSearch.com
Wize.com

Support and Info for Parents of Multiples
Mothers of SuperTwins: MOSTonline.org
National Organization of Mothers of Twins Clubs:
    nomotc.org

TripletConnection.org
TwinsMagazine.com

Universal Baby Registries
MyRegistry.com
www.amazon.com/gp/registry/universal

Nursery Design Inspiration
Ohdeedoh.com
ProjectNursery.com

DIY and Handmade Baby Stuff
Etsy.com
Make-Baby-Stuff.com
PrudentBaby.com

Breastfeeding Info and Support
Cerean Breastfeeding: cerean.net
KellyMom.com
La Leche League International: llli.org

Homemade Baby Food Recipes
Weelicious.com
WholesomeBabyFood.com

Cloth Diapering Info and Bargains
ClothDiaperFoundation.org

DiaperJungle.com
DiaperPin.com
DiaperSewing.com
DiaperSwappers.com

Baby Carrier Info and Discounts
DaintyBaby.com
For Sale or Trade forum at TheBabyWearer.com
FrogMama.com

Appendix B
Smart Products to Put on
Your Baby Registry

• • •

10 Baby "Needs" Worth Registering For
- Crib
- Crib mattress
- Crib bedding
- Diapers (cloth or disposable)/wipes
- Formula (if you plan to use it)
- Breast pump
- Bottles
- Disposable or washable breast pads
- Car seat
- Baby thermometer

10 Popular Extras Worth Registering For
- Baby carrier
- Stroller
- Portable play yard

- Bouncer
- Swing
- Diaper bag
- Diaper pail
- Baby monitors
- Nursing cover
- Swaddling blankets or swaddling gowns

Popular Extras for Later On
- High chair
- Baby food storage jars
- Umbrella stroller
- Baby-proofing items

Other Really Cool Things to "Register" For
- Gift cards to photo print and gift Web sites
- Homemade meals for the freezer
- Gift certificates for something to make a new mom feel pampered (manicure, haircut, and so on)
- Gift certificate for an hour of babysitting

Index

• • •

Activity centers/mats, 22, 276, 284–88
aden + anais, 205
Adiri Natural Nurser, 132
Advertising, xiii, 5–7, 16, 26, 35, 273
AFullCup.com, 43, 77–78
Agriculture, U.S. Department of, xiii
Air purifiers, 88
AlbeeBaby.com, 230
All-in-One diapers (AIOs), 148–49
Amazon.com, 30, 33, 37, 47, 48, 91, 104, 106, 120, 122, 127, 129, 137, 195, 207, 214, 215, 230, 263, 267, 279
Amazon Mom, 39
   Subscribe & Save discount, 124, 157, 165, 167, 179
Ameda Purely Yours Breast Pump, 117
American Academy of Pediatrics, 84, 90
   Healthy Child site, 226, 291
American Automobile Association (AAA), 161
American Baby crib sheet, 96
Anita nursing bras, 121
Antibacterial surface wipes, 176, 177
Artwork, in nursery, 99–100, 112

Asian soft carriers, 250–51
AskDrSears.com, 84
Aveeno.com, 192, 193

Babe Safe, 94
Babies (documentary), 3
Babies "R"Us, 29, 54, 160, 267
   Especially for Baby Stacking Cups, 284
Babies "R"Us Registry, 11, 47
Baby bath products (*See* Bath time)
BabyBjörn
   baby carriers, 252
   bouncers, 266
BabyCall monitor (Sony), 108
Baby carriers, 235, 239, 247–56
   cost of, 252–53
   coupons, 253
   covers and ponchos for, 255
   favorite, 251–52
   reader tips, 248–49, 255
   sales, 253
   secondhand, 253, 256
   sling safety, 254
   types of, 247–48, 250–51
BabyCenter.com, 146
BabyCheapskate.com, xv, 36–37, 99, 129, 157, 160, 164, 173, 212
Baby clubs, 67
Baby Einstein, 276, 285

Baby food, 22
  commercial, 136–37
  coupons for, 66–67
  homemade, 134–36, 143
  organic, 137–38
Baby gear, 257–72
  bassinets, 11, 259–63, 269–70
  bouncers, 263, 265–68, 271, 272
  cradles, 269
  Moses baskets, 269–70
  play yards, 258–63, 271
  rockers, 268–69, 272
  swings, 257–58, 263–68, 271–72
Baby gyms, 274–76
BabyHawk Mei Tai, 250
Baby Jogger, 34
  City Mini Double stroller, 240, 246
  City Mini stroller, 241, 244
BabyLegs, 206
Baby Mod, 92
Baby monitors, 107–8, 111
Baby product industry, 4–5, 16–17, 26, 107
Baby-proofing equipment, 22
Baby registry, 45–55 (*see also* Baby showers)
  at consignment stores, 59
  discounted leftover items on, 46–47
  essential items, 49
  gift cards, 51, 52
  higher-priced items, 50, 86, 93, 200
  most popular places, 47
  for multiples, 54–55
  number of items, 53–54
  reader tips, 52–53
  10 baby "needs," 50, 301
  10 popular extras, 301–2
  universal, 48–49
Baby showers, xvi, 15, 46, 56
  board book showers, 290
  family members and, 57
  "handmade," 58
  ideas for, 58–59
  returning gifts, 59, 60

"secondhand," 58–59
  thank-you notes for, 59
  timing of, 57
BabySteals.com, 35, 151, 173, 253
Baby swings, 12, 17–18, 22, 257–58, 263–68, 271–72
Baby Trend
  Expedition sport stroller, 243
  Flex-Loc car seat, 231
  play yard, 262
  Snap N Go car seat stroller, 243
TheBabyWearer.com, 248, 253
Bare Naked Boppy, 120
TheBargainWatcher.com, 19
Bassinets, 11, 259–63, 269–70
Bath time, 185–96
  reader tips, 186–88
  samples and coupons, 16
  soaps and shampoos, 191–93
  sponge baths, 185, 186
  towels, 193–94
  toys, 194–95, 196
  tubs, 186–90, 196
  tub spout covers, 191
BébéPOD, 270–71
Beckham, Victoria, 81
Beco Butterfly II baby carrier, 251
Bedding, 11, 12, 95–97, 111
Beech-Nut, 66, 137
Better Business Bureau, 74
Binge spending, 23
Birth announcements, 4
BJ's Wholesale Club, 38
Blankets, 12
Blinds, in nursery, 101–2, 112
Blocks, 274
Board book showers, 290
BOB, 34, 240
  Revolution SE Duallie stroller, 246
  Revolution SE stroller, 244
  Revolution stroller, 241
Bodysuits, 206–7
Bookcases, in nursery, 106, 111
Books, 289–90

Boon, 195
Booster seats, 56, 139, 142
Boppy pillow, 120, 121
Bottles, 12, 115, 124, 131–32, 142
Bouncers, 12, 13, 17–18, 263, 265–
    68, 271, 272
BPA (bisphenol A), 118, 132, 190,
    191, 195, 281
BrandSaver coupon insert, 68, 160
Bravado nursing bras and tanks,
    121, 122–23
Breastfeeding, 11–12, 113–25
    accessories, 120–25
    bottles and, 115, 124
    breast pads, 115, 123–24, 142
    milk storage containers, 115, 124
    nursing bras, 115, 121–22, 142
    nursing covers, 125, 142
    nursing tops and tanks, 122–23,
        142
    pillow, 120–21, 142
    pumps (see Breast pumps)
Breast pumps, 12, 142
    advantages of, 115
    double electric, 116–17, 119
    hospital-grade, 116
    manual, 117–18
    reader tip, 117
    secondhand, 118
    single electric, 117
BreastPumpsDirect.com, 120
Bright Starts
    activity centers/mats, 276, 285
    Comfort & Harmony Portable
        Swing, 265
    Rattle and Shake Barbell Rattle,
        282
Britax, 38
    Boulevard 70 car seat, 233
    Chaperone car seat, 231
    Marathon 70 car seat, 233
Bugaboo stroller, 235–36
Bumbo Baby Sitter, 270– 271
bumGenius 4.0, 148
Bumkins, 149

Bumpers, 96–97
Burt's Bees Baby Wash, 192
Buy Buy Baby, 47, 230
Buying behavior, 4, 7–8
Buzzillions.com, 29

California Baby's Super Sensitive
    products, 192
Calmoseptine, 182
CamelCamel-Camel.com, 33
Carriers (see Baby carriers)
Car-Safety.org, 226
Car seat covers, 203
Car Seat Lady, The, 226
CarSeat.org, 226, 228
Car seats, 12, 38, 54, 221–34
    convertible, 223, 229, 231–33
    cost of, 228–30
    coupons, 230
    expiration dates, 224, 225
    infant, 223, 229, 231–32
    installation, 225, 234
    LATCH (Lower Anchors and
        Tethers for CHildren) system,
        224
    reader tips, 227–28, 232
    safety resources, 226
    sales, 230
    secondhand, 14, 225, 234
    winter coats and, 204
Carter's, 36, 213
    bodysuits, 207, 210
    Easy Fit crib sheet, 96
Cellfire.com, 72
Centers for Disease Control
    (CDC), 155
Changing tables, pads, and covers,
    83, 105–6, 111, 259–63
Changing time, 169–84
    diaper bags (see Diaper bags)
    diaper pails, 177–80, 183
    diaper rash, 181–83, 184
    portable pad/mat, 176–77
    public restrooms and, 176–77
    reader tip, 180

Chemical exposure, 87–88, 98
Chicco
    Cortina stroller, 230, 240, 241,
        244
    Cortina Together Double
        stroller, 246
    Ct0.6 Capri umbrella stroller,
        242
    KeyFit 30 car seat, 230–32, 244
Child of Mine mobiles, 99
Child Passenger Safety Inspection
    Station, 225
Children's Place, The, 36, 67, 213
Circo (Target)
    clothing, 213
    crib sheet, 96
City Mini Double stroller, 240
Closeouts, 35, 38
Closet space, 84
Clothdiaperfoundation.org, 152
Cloth diapers, 11, 54, 146–53, 167,
    182
Clothing, 12, 197–218
    amount needed, 204, 218
    from baby shower, 52, 59
    bodysuits, 206–7
    drool bibs, 206
    favorite brands and stores,
        212–13
    flame retardants, 209
    freebies, 197–99
    garment extenders, 207
    hangers, 201
    layette, 200–9
    leg and arm warmers, 206
    for multiples, 207–8
    online shopping, 212, 214
    organic, 209–10
    reader tips, 202–3, 205, 207–8,
        212
    reselling, 198, 216–17, 218
    sales, 198, 214, 215
    secondhand, 17, 198
    shoes, 213–16, 218
    sizes, 210

    stocking up on, 211–12, 218
    summer, 202–3
    washing, 213
    wearable blankets, 205–6
    winter, 202–4
Cloth wipes, 166
Clouds and Stars QuickZip Sheet,
    96
Colgate Eco Classica I Crib
    Mattress, 95
Combi Shuttle 33 car seat, 231
Consignment sales and stores, 18,
    19, 34, 59, 86, 87, 141, 174, 201,
    208, 216–17, 240, 267, 271, 276,
    277
Consumer Product Safety
    Commission (CPSC), 84, 190,
    254, 261
Consumer Product Safety
    Improvement Act (CPSIA),
    98
Consumer Reports, 93
ConsumerSearch.com, 29
Convertible car seats, 223, 229,
    231–33
Convertible cribs, 91
Cornstarch, 182, 183
Cosco
    Fold Flat high chair, 141
    Funsport, 263
    Scenera 40RF car seat, 232
Cosleepers, 11, 269
Cosleeping, 84
Costco, 38, 129
Cotton sheets, 95–96
CouponClippers.com, 77
Coupon codes, 42, 44, 71
    decoding, 70
Couponing forums, 43
Coupons, xv, 5–7, 9, 16, 21, 36,
    61–78
    baby bath products, 192, 196
    baby carriers, 253
    baby clubs, 67
    baby food, 136–37

basics about, 62–63
best sources, 65–72
breast milk storage containers,
    115, 124
car seats, 230
clipping services, 77
diapers, 16, 36, 66, 68, 154,
    159–60
double and triple, 76
formula, 16, 66, 126–27,
    142–43
mail or e-mail sign-ups, 66–67
manufacturer's, 62–63, 67, 68,
    74
mobile coupons, 71–72
newspaper inserts, 68, 160
printable, 68, 69, 160
reader tips, 64, 68, 71
store, 62–63, 67, 74
terms, 64–65
Coupons.com, 68, 127, 160
CouponSherpa.com, 72
Coupon-trading groups, 77
Cradles, 269
Craigslist.org, 15, 19, 86, 87, 105,
    118, 141, 151, 174, 199, 240, 267,
    271
Crazy8, 67
Cribs, 11
baby registry and, 50, 86
convertible, 91
cost of, 91–92, 110
mattresses, 92–95, 111
mobiles, 98–99, 111
for multiples, 109
safety issues, 90
secondhand, 89–90
sheets, 95–97, 111
shopping for, 91
size of, 83
waterproof crib mattress pads,
    97–98, 111
Crib soothers, 274, 275
Curtains, in nursery, 101–2, 112
CVS, 69, 73

Daily deal sites, 75–76
Dainty Baby.com, 253
DaVinci crib, 92
Diaper bags, 16–17
contents of, 174–76
cost of, 171–73
men and, 170
reader tips, 175
secondhand, 174, 183
Diaper Champ, 178, 179
Diaper Dekor, 178
Diaper Dude backpacks, 173
Diaper ointment, 16
Diaper pails, 177–80, 183
DiaperPin.com, 147
Diaper rash, 181–83, 184
Diapers, 11, 21, 49, 145–64 (see also
    Changing time)
amount needed, 150, 155–57
baby showers and, 58
bags (see Diaper bags)
cloth, 11, 54, 146–53, 167, 182
cost of, xiv, 147, 150, 153–55, 163
coupons for, 16, 36, 66, 68, 154,
    159–60
disposable, 11, 54, 146–47,
    153–64
environmentally friendly, 162–63
fit and sizing, 154–55
fitted, 148
as gifts, 146
liners, 153
multiples and, 54
one-size, 147–48
premium, 158–59
reader tips, 151–52, 157
sales, 151, 157–59, 161–62, 164, 167
samples, 16, 36
secondhand cloth, 151, 167
size of packages of, 153–54
store-brand, 163–64, 167
trial programs, 150
at warehouse clubs, 39
Diapers.com, 29
Diaper sprayer, 152

Diono Radian XTSL car seat, 233
Discounts, xiv, 23, 35, 37 (*see also* Coupons)
   on leftover registry items, 46–47
   multiples and, 54–55
Disposable diapers, 11, 54, 146–47, 153–64
Dr. Bronner's soap, 192
Dr. Brown's Natural Flow bottle, 132
Dr. Sears Web site, 123
Double coupons, 76
Double electric breast pumps, 116–17, 119
Dressers, in nursery, 105, 111
Driving costs, 161–62, 167
Drool bibs, 206
Drugstore.com, 29
Dutailier, 104

Earth's Best
   baby food, 69, 137, 138
   diapers, 159, 162
   organic formula, 127
eBay, 20, 87, 128, 151, 174, 289
eBayClassifieds.com, 19
Eco-foam mattresses, 93
Eddie Bauer diaper bags, 171
eeBoo Tot Towers Nesting Boxes, 284
8coupons.com, 71
Emotional spending, 7
Enfamil, 66, 125, 128, 130, 171
Entertainment centers, 274
ERGObaby carrier, 34, 251–53
eToys.com, 29
Etsy.com, 48, 99, 100, 152, 180
Evenflo
   activity centers, 284
   Tribute 5 car seat, 233
   Triumph 65 LX car seat, 233
Evernote.com, 28
Eversave.com, 75
ExerSaucer (activity center), 22, 284–85, 288

Expedit line, IKEA, 106
Expiration dates, of car seats, 224, 225

Facebook, xvi, 36, 40, 42–44, 69, 70, 192, 241, 253
Federal Trade Commission (FTC), 74
Feeding baby, (*see also* Baby food; Breastfeeding; Formula)
   high chairs, 22, 56, 138–42
First Years, 54
   Ignite umbrella stroller, 243
   Infant to Toddler Tub with Sling, 189
   True Fit car seat, 232
Fisher-Price
   activity mats, 276
   bouncers, 266
   Brilliant Basics Baby's First Blocks, 283
   Brilliant Basics Stack & Roll Cups, 284
   Cradle Swing, 265
   crib soothers, 275
   Healthy Care Deluxe Booster Seat, 139
   high chairs, 139, 141
   Infant to Toddler Rocker, 269
   Jumperoo, 287
   Laugh & Learn Fun with Friends, 279–80
   Laugh & Learn Learning Home, 279
   Laugh & Learn Learning Kitchen, 279
   Little Superstar Classical Stacker, 284
   mobiles, 99
   Newborn Rock 'n Play Sleeper, 268
   Open-Top Cradle Swing, 265
   Precious Planet Whale of a Tub, 189

Rainforest Cradle Swing, 267
Rock-a-Stack, 284
Space Saver high chair, 139
Stride-to-Ride Lion, 280
Take Along Swing, 265
Flame retardants, 209
Flensted mobiles, 99
Fleurville diaper bags, 173
Fleurville fabric, 171
Flip diapers, 149
FLOR carpet tiles, 102
Foam mattresses, 93
Food and Drug Administration
(FDA), 118
Formula
cost of, xiv, 125–26
coupons, 16, 66, 126–27, 142–43
organic, 127
reader tip, 131
samples, 16, 130
specialty, 128
store-brand, 128–29
at warehouse clubs, 39
where to buy, 129–30
Foursquare.com, 72
Freebies, 5, 12–17
Freebies4Mom.com, 41
Freecycle.org, 14–15, 105, 141, 174,
188, 199, 267, 289
Friends and Family sales, 36, 37
FrogMama.com, 253
FSA (flexible spending account),
119
Full-sized stroller, 237
FuzziBunz diapers, 148, 151

Gap, the, 36, 213
Garage sales, 18, 19, 240, 289
Garment extenders, 207
gDiapers, 149
Gear (see Baby gear)
Gerber, 66, 137, 210
breast milk storage bags, 124
diaper bags, 171
GetYowza.com, 72

Gift bag advertising, 5–6, 16
Gift cards, 51, 52
Gilligen & O'Malley nursing tanks,
123
Glamourmom nursing tanks,
122–23
Glass bottles, 131
GoodGuide.com, 87
GoodStart, 66
formula, 125
Goodwill, 200, 289
Google Product Search, 31
Google Shopper, 31
Graco
activity centers, 285
activity mats, 276
Alano stroller, 243
Contempo high chair, 141
diaper bags, 171
DuoDiner high chair, 142
Duoglider LX stroller, 246
Lauren crib, 30–31, 92
LiteRider stroller, 243
Lovin Hug Swing, 265
Mealtime high chair, 141
MetroLite stroller, 244
Pack 'n Play, 262
Quattro Tour Deluxe stroller,
244
Quattro Tour Duo stroller, 246
Travel Lite Crib, 262
Twin IPO umbrella stroller, 245
GreenGuard.org, 87
Green Toys My First Stacker, 284
GroceryIQ.com, 72
Groupon.com, 75
GroVia diapers, 149
Growth charts, 155, 156, 223
Gymboree clothing, 210, 213

HABA Kringelring, 281
Halo, 205
Hand sanitizer, 176, 177
Hands-free nursing bras, 122
Hangers, 201

HappyBaby, 67, 137, 138
HappyHeinys diapers, 148
HealthyChild.org, 87
Helping Hands for Special Kids, 128
High chairs, 22, 56, 138–42
Hive.BurtsBees.com, 193
Home Depot, 103
Homemade baby food, 134–36, 143
Homemade wipes, 166
Hooded bath towels, 194
Hospital-grade breast pumps, 116
HotCouponWorld.com, 43, 77
Huggies, 54, 66, 68, 158–60, 163, 165
Hybrid diapers, 149

IKEA, 88–89, 91, 92, 102, 104–6, 109
Impulse spending, avoidance of, 7–9, 39, 40
Infant car seat carrier, 237
Infant car seats, 223, 229, 231–32
Infantino
    activity mats, 276
    Barn Shape Sorter, 283
    Eco Sash Wrap & Tie Soft Baby Carrier, 254
    Fold and Go Bouncer, 266
Innerspring mattresses, 93
Instant rebates, 74
i play, 195, 206

Jeep
    Cherokee Sport stroller, 243
    diaper bags, 171
Jersey sheets, 95–96
JJ Cole
    fleece buntings, 203
    Mode diaper bags, 173
Jogger stroller, 237, 238
Johnson & Johnson, 192
JohnsonsBaby.com, 193
Jumperoo, 22, 287, 288

Jumpers, 287
Juvenile Product Manufacturers Association (JPMA) certification, 90, 93, 190

KidsConsignmentSales.com, 19
Kid to Kid (kidtokid.com), 19, 217
Kissaluv diapers, 148, 149
Kohl's, 207
Kolcraft, 30
    Contours Lite stroller, 20, 243
    Contours Options Tandem stroller, 246
    Contours Options 3-Wheel II stroller, 245
Kroger, 69, 73
Kushies changing pad, 177

Lamaze
    Jacques the Peacock, 282
    Mortimer the Moose, 282
Land's End diaper bags, 171
Lansinoh
    Affinity Double Electric Breast Pump, 117
    breast milk storage bags, 124
    disposable breast pads, 123
LATCH (Lower Anchors and Tethers for CHildren) system, 224
Latex nipples, 133
Layette, 200–9
Lead-based paint, 87
LeapFrog
    Learn and Groove Table, 280
    My Pal Scout/Violet, 280
Leg and arm warmers, 206
Lifefactoy Multi-Sensory Silicone Teether, 281
Lighting, in nursery, 104, 112
Lightweight stroller, 237
LilyPadz washable pads, 123
LivingSocial.com, 75
Liz Lange nursing tanks, 123

Lorex monitors, 108
Lowe's, 103
Loyalty cards, 73

Maclaren
    bouncers, 266
    Techno XT stroller, 244
    Triumph stroller, 241, 244–45
    Twin Techno stroller, 245
    Twin Triumph stroller, 245
    Volo umbrella stroller, 241,
        243
Magazine advertisements, xiii, 26
Mail-in rebates, 73–74
Make and Takes, 194
Make-Baby-Stuff.com, 97, 121
Malm line, 105
Mamabargains.com, 173
MamboSprouts.com, 69
Manhattan Toy mobiles, 99
Manhattan Toy Winkel, 281
Manual breast pumps, 117–18
Manufacturer's coupons, 62–63, 67,
        68, 74
Manufacturer's minimum
        advertised price (MAP),
        34–35, 253
Manufacturer's suggested retail
        price
        (MSRP), 30
MAP pricing, 34–35, 253
Maternity clothing, 6, 20
Mattresses, crib, 92–95, 111
Maya Wrap, 250
Medela, 34, 54
    disposable breast pads, 123
    Harmony Breast Pump, 118
    Pump in Style Advanced, 116,
        117, 118
MeetUp.com, 20
Mei Tai baby carrier, 250–51, 254
Melissa & Doug Wooden Shape
        Sorting Clock, 283
Mirrors, 274, 275
Mobile coupons, 71–72

Mobiles, crib, 98–99, 111, 274, 275
Moby Wrap, 251, 252
Monitors, 107–8, 111
Moonlight Slumber Eco-Friendly
        Little Dreamer One Firmness
        All Foam Crib Mattress, 95
Moses baskets, 269–70
MOST (Mothers of SuperTwins),
        55
Motherhood Maternity, 6, 124
Mothers or Parents of Multiples,
        55, 208
MULA Stack n Nest Cups, 284
Multiples
    clothing for, 207–8
    diaper use of, 54
    nursery for, 108–10
    reader tips, 55–56
    registry and, 54–55
Munchkin Mozart Magic Cube,
        280
Murals, in nursery, 100–1
Music, 290–91
My Brest Friend, 120
MyRegistry.com, 48–49

National Highway Traffic Safety
        Administration (NHTSA),
        222
    Child Safety site, 226
National Organization of Mothers
        of Twins Clubs, 55
Nature Babycare, 162–63
Naturepedic's No Compromise crib
        mattress, 93
Nature's Goodness (Del Monte),
        66, 137
Needs
    two types of, 6–7
    versus wants, 11–12
Nestlé, 125
Newspaper coupon inserts, 68,
        160
Nipples, 12, 132–33, 142
NoBetterDeal.com, 267, 268

Nursery, setting up, 12, 81–112
  artwork, 99–100, 112
  baby monitors, 107–8, 111
  basic ideas, 82–83
  bookcases, 106, 111
  changing tables, pads, and
    covers, 83, 105–6, 111
  color schemes, 85
  cribs (*see* Cribs)
  curtains and blinds, 101–2, 112
  dressers, 105, 111
  going green, 87–88
  lighting, 104, 112
  for multiples, 108–10
  murals and wall decals, 100–1
  overspending, 81
  paint, 102–3
  reader tips, 94, 96–97, 99, 110
  rockers and gliders, 103–4, 111
  rugs, 102, 112
  secondhand items, 86–88
  space-maximizing tips, 83–84
  storage, 104–5, 109
Nursing (*see* Breastfeeding)
Nursing bras, 115, 121–22, 142
Nursing covers, 125, 142
Nursing tops and tanks, 122–23, 142

Ohdeedoh.com, 83, 85
OiOi fabric, 171
Old Navy, 36, 210, 213
Olivia crib, 92
Once Upon a Child
  (onceuponachild.com), 19
Online sources, 13–15, 19, 20, 29,
  46, 48, 160 (*see also* specific
  websites)
Organic clothing, 209–10
Organic formula, 127
Organic products, 69
Organics by Tadpoles, 210
OshKosh B'Gosh, 36, 213
Outgassing of VOCs, 87–88, 94
Outings, 292
Overstock.com, 29, 91, 105

Pack 'n Play, 109, 259–60
Paint
  lead-based, 87
  in nursery, 102–3
Pampers, 54, 66, 68, 158–60, 165
Pandora.com, 291
PaperBackSwap.com, 290
Parenting, Inc. (Paul), 235, 293
Parenting books, 113
Parenting magazines, 5
Parents Healthy Kids Sampler, 6
ParkLane crib, 92
Paul, Pamela, 235, 293
PaxBaby.com, 248
PBDEs, 209
PeaPod travel bed, 262
Pediped shoes, 215
Pedoodles shoes, 216
Peekaru Original baby carrier
  cover, 255
Personal recommendations, 28, 29
Pesticides, 127, 209
Petunia Pickle Bottom, 173
Philips AVENT
  baby monitors, 108
  bottles, 132
  BPA-Free Manual Breast Pump,
    118
  disposable breast pads, 123
  Range BPA-Free Front Teeth
    Teether, 281
Phthalates, 98, 190, 195
Physiological needs, 11, 12
Pillows, breastfeeding, 120–21, 142
Piperlime.com, 214
Planet Wise, 180
Plastic bottles, 131
Playskool Busy Ball Popper, 279
Playtex
  BPA-free Drop-Ins Original
    bottle, 132
  breast milk storage bags, 124
  Diaper Genie II Elite, 178, 179
  nursing bras, 121
  VentAire Advanced bottle, 132

Play yards, 12, 258–63, 271
Plum Organics, 138
Poang chair, 104
Pocket diapers, 148
Polyurethane foam, 87
Ponijao, 3
PortableBaby.com, 248
Portable changing pad/mat, 176–77
Potty-training, 145
Pouches, 250
Premium wipes, 165
Pressed wood furniture, 87
Price Chopper Baby Club, 67
Price comparison search engine, 31
Prices, tracking, 30–33
Primo EuroBath Tub, 189
Prince Lionheart
    BébéPOD, 270
    washPOD, 189, 190
Printable coupons, 68, 69, 160
Procter & Gamble, 68
Product recalls, 14, 18, 41
Product reviews, 28–29
ProjectNursery.com, 85
PrudentBaby.com, 97, 125, 194
Psychological needs, 7
Publix Baby Club, 67

Radio advertising, 35
Rainforest Healthy Care Booster
    Seat, 139
Rattles, 22, 274, 276, 282
Raz-baby RaZBerry Teether, 281
Rebates, 23, 73–74
Recaro ProRIDE car seat, 233
ReCrib.com, 20
RedLaser (redlaser.com), 31
Registry (see Baby registry)
REI.com, 29
Repurposing items, 15–16, 17, 82,
    85–86, 277
Research, 26–30
Reselling, 23, 198, 216–17, 218,
    268

Restrooms, public, 176–77
RetailMeNot.com, 70
Return policy, 46, 47
Rice cereal, 134
Ride-on stroller, 237
Ring slings, 250
Rite Aid, 73
Robeez shoes, 215
Rockers, baby, 268–69, 272
Rockers and gliders, in nursery,
    103–4, 111
Rookie-Moms.com, 292
Rugs, in nursery, 102, 112

SafeMama.com, 87, 136, 195
Safety 1st
    Complete 65 LX car seat, 233
    onBoard 35 Air car seat, 231
    play yard, 262
Sales, 21
    baby carriers, 253
    car seats, 230
    closeouts, 35, 38
    clothing, 198, 214, 215
    diaper bags, 172–73
    diapers, 151, 157–59, 161–62,
        164, 167
    finding out about, 35–38
    formula, 126, 129
    predicting, 37–38
    seasonal, 37
    social media and, 40–43
    store clearance sales, 37
    strollers, 240–41
    10 popular extras, 51
    toys, 278
    tracking prices, 30–31
Samples, 4–7, 16
    baby bath products, 192, 196
    formula, 130
Sam's Club, 38, 164
Sassy, 191, 195
    Rattlin Rings, 282
Save-a-Lot Being Well Baby Club,
    67

Saving, 3–23, (*see also* Sales;
    Secondhand items)
  five basic principles of, 10–23
  goals, 8–9
  types of savers, 9–10
  warehouse clubs and, 38–40
See Kai Run shoes, 215
Sealy Soybean Foam-Core Crib
    Mattress, 95
Seasonal sales, 37
Secondhand items, 35
  baby carriers, 253, 256
  baby shower and, 58–59
  bathtubs, 188, 196
  bouncers/swings, 267
  breast pumps, 118
  Bumbos and bébéPODs, 271
  car seats, 14, 225, 234
  cloth diapers, 151, 167
  clothing, 17, 198
  comfort zone for, 18
  crib mattresses, 94
  cribs, 89–90
  diaper bags, 174, 183
  diaper pails, 179
  dressers, 105
  high chairs, 141
  for multiples, 56
  for nursery, 86–88
  play yards, 261
  recalls on, 14, 18, 261
  sources for, 19–20
  strollers, 240, 256
  toys, 277, 285, 287
  waterproof crib mattress pads,
    98
Serta Nightstar Eco Firm Crib and
    Toddler Mattress, 95
Seventh Generation, 66
  diapers, 159, 162
Shampoos, 191–93
Shape sorters, 282–83
Sheets, crib, 95–97, 111
Shermag, 104
Shipping gifts, 46

Shoes, 213–16, 218
Shoes.com, 214
ShopLocal.com, 36
Shopping (*see also* Sales)
  product reviews, 28–29
  researching prior to, 26–30
ShopRite Baby Bucks, 67
ShopSavvy (shopsavvy.mobi), 31
Shortcuts.com, 160
Showers (*see* Baby showers)
Silicone nipples, 133
Similac, 66, 125, 130, 171
Simple Wishes Hands Free
    Breastpump
    Bra, 122
Single electric breast pumps, 117
6pm.com, 214
Skip Hop, 191
  diaper bags, 172
Sleep
  cosleeping, 11, 84, 269
  cribs (*see* Cribs)
Sleep bras, 121–22
SlickDeals.net, 43
Slings, 250, 254
SmartSource.com, 68, 160
SmartSource coupon insert, 68
Soaps, 191–93
Social needs, 7
TheSoftLanding.com, 190, 195
Solid food (*see* Baby food)
Sony BabyCall monitor, 108
Specialty formula, 128
Spending diary, 8
Sponge baths, 185, 186
Sprout, 67, 137, 138
Squeakers shoes, 216
Stacking and sorting toys, 283–84
Standard stroller, 237
Starter kits, 16
Stokke Xplory stroller, 236
Storage, in nursery, 83–84, 104–5,
    109
Store brands, 23
  diapers, 163–64, 167

formula, 128–29
wipes, 165
Store circulars, 35, 36, 43
Store clearance sales, 37
Store coupons, 62–63, 67, 74
Store loyalty cards, 73
Stork Craft
    crib, 92
    glider, 104
Storksak, 171
Stride Rite shoes, 215
Strollers, 12, 235–47, 256
    best strollers over $100, 244–45
    best strollers under $100, 242–43
    must-have list of features,
        239–40
    reader tips, 246–47
    sales, 240–41
    secondhand, 240, 256
    tandem and double, 245–47
    types of, 237
Sumersault crib sheet, 96
Summer Infant, 205
    Best View and Day and Night
        video monitors, 108
    changing pad, 177
    contoured changing pad, 106
    Ultimate Crib Sheet, 96
Survey responses, 4
SwapBabyGoods.com, 20, 211
SwapMamas.com, 20
Swap meets, 19–20
Swings, 12, 17–18, 22, 257–58,
    263–68, 271–72
Synthetic carpet, 87

Tandem strollers, 245–47
Target, 30, 33, 38, 40, 47, 67, 69, 71,
    91, 102, 105, 120, 121, 123, 129,
    137, 160, 164, 165, 172, 195,
    207, 210, 213–15, 230, 263, 267,
    279
Teethers, 22, 281
Television advertising, 35, 273
Television viewing, 291

Temptation-avoidance techniques,
    7–9
Thirsties, 148
ThredUp.com, 20
Thrift stores, 18, 19, 124, 199–200,
    201
Time magazine, 81
Tiny Love
    activity mats, 276
    Gymini Bouncer, 266
    mobiles, 99
TLC television show, 10, 62
Towels, 193–94
Toys, 273–94
    activity centers/mats, 22, 276,
        284–88
    baby gyms, 274–76
    bath time, 194–95, 196
    blocks, 274
    books, 289–90
    crib soothers, 274, 275
    entertainment centers, 274
    for five to twelve months,
        278–80
    mirrors, 274, 275
    mobiles, 98–99, 111, 274, 275
    music, 290–91
    rattles, 274, 276, 282
    reader tips, 288
    sales, 278
    saving money on, 277–78
    secondhand, 277, 285, 287
    shape sorters, 282–83
    stacking and sorting, 283–84
    teethers, 281
Travel costs, 40
Trend Lab diaper bags, 171
Triple coupons, 76
Triplet Connection, 55
Tub spout covers, 191
Tubs (*see* Bath time)
Tummy Tub, 189, 190
Tupperware Shape O, 283
Tushies, 163
Twins (*see* Multiples)

Twins magazine, 55
Twitter, 4, 40–42, 44, 70

Umbrella stroller, 237
Universal registries, 48–49
UPC code(s), 73
UPPABaby G-Lite umbrella
    stroller, 244

Valassis (RedPlum) coupon insert,
    68
Vaseline, 183
Video monitors, 108
Videos, 292
Vinyl (PVC), 87, 98, 190
Volatile organic compounds
    (VOCs), 87, 102, 103
Vouchers, 75–76
Vulli's Sophie the Giraffe, 281

Wall decals, in nursery, 100–1
Walmart, 30, 33, 91, 92, 99, 102,
    120, 121, 129, 137, 164, 210,
    230, 263, 267, 279
Walt Disney Company, 197–98
Wants, versus needs, 11–12
Warehouse clubs, 38–40, 129, 164

Waterproof covers, 87, 97–98, 111,
    148
Wearable blankets, 205–6
Weelicious.com, 136
Welcome kits, 5, 6, 16
Wet bag, 152–53, 180
WeUseCoupons.com, 78
White noise, 88
Whole Foods, 69
WholesomeBabyFood.com, 135–36
WIC Program, 119, 128
Winn-Dixie Baby Club, 67
Wipes, 11
    amount needed, 164
    coupons for, 16, 66
    premium versus store-brand,
        165–66, 167
    reader tip, 165–66
    samples, 16
Wize.com, 29
Wrap baby carriers, 251

Yard sales, 19, 86, 141, 267

Zavers.com, 72
ZingSale.com, 33
Zulily.com, 35, 173